# BUILDING AN ENTERPRISE ARCHITECTURE PRACTICE

# THE ENTERPRISE SERIES

*The titles published in this series are listed at the end of this volume.*

# Building an Enterprise Architecture Practice

Tools, Tips, Best Practices,
Ready-to-Use Insights

*by*

MARTIN VAN DEN BERG

*and*

MARLIES VAN STEENBERGEN

 Springer

A C.I.P. Catalogue record for this book is available from the Library of Congress.

ISBN-10 1-4020-5605-2 (HB)
ISBN-13 978-1-4020-5605-5 (HB)
ISBN-10 1-4020-5606-0 (e-book)
ISBN-13 978-1-4020-5606-2 (e-book)

Published by Springer,
P.O. Box 17, 3300 AA Dordrecht, The Netherlands.

*www.springer.com*

*Printed on acid-free paper*

# ACCLAIM FOR BUILDING AN ENTERPRISE ARCHITECTURE PRACTICE

*"Enterprise Architecture has been an 'emerging' discipline for quite some time now, with a plethora of literature repeatedly providing mostly theoretical speculations. This book fills the urgent need of providing a pragmatic approach to converting those theories into a meaningful, viable, and useful architecture practice within an enterprise. In addition to addressing the key aspects of an architecture practice, the book also offers several valuable tools, such as the DYA Model and the Architecture Maturity Matrix, helping tailor and develop the most suitable architecture strategy for a given enterprise."*

Atul Bhatt, Ph.D.
Enterprise Architect in the financial services industry

---

*"DYA is THE practical framework for architects. It focuses on the process and deliverables of the architectural services. DYA gives suggestions how EA can be structured, but it's up to the organisation to choose any EA framework as base for DYA. This book gives, by way of examples and best practices, guidelines how to implement the architectural processes and outlines the services an architect should deliver.*
*The philosophy DYA drums into the reader, 'just enough, just in time,' appeals to us. When addressing EA, don't grasp it in one bite. Do it the DYA way, bit by bit in a structured and controlled manner, just enough just in time. In other words, grow with Dynamic Enterprise Architecture."*

Örjan Carlsson
Chief Architect at the national board of student aid in Sweden, CSN

---

*"The previous book on DYA, Dynamic Enterprise Architecture: How to Make it Work, has been used with great success for several years now in the IT-bachelors program of the Hogeschool of Amsterdam. This new book is a worthy successor. It provides our students with methods to implement the architectural function in various*

kinds of companies. It gives them a broad vision on what is required to successfully implement an enterprise architecture practice."

Jan Hellings
Tutor Information Technology, Hogeschool van Amsterdam

---

"*This book is a must-read for Architects, as it describes in a very clear and pragmatic way how to successfully develop an agile Architecture which provides actual value to your business. Furthermore, it provides a practical and powerful approach to measuring and improving the maturity of Architecture thinking and working within you organization.*"

Johan Nelis
Author of the book *Business Process Management, Practical Guidelines for Successful Implementation*

---

"*Martin van den Berg and Marlies van Steenbergen have created a practical handbook that can serve as an Enterprise Architecture foundation to help organisations in planning and organising their Enterprise Architecture efforts. Trying to understand the different elements described in this book, is one step, translating them to your own situation is another step. This book is a must read for organisations that have the ambition to take Enterprise Architecture serious and are trying to increase their EA professionalism.*"

Jaap Schekkerman B.Sc.
President & Thought Leader Institute For Enterprise Architecture Developments

---

"*This book gives the reader a comprehensive holistic view on enterprise architecture and the importance of priorities in the architecture process. It shows very concrete steps and practical guidelines how to deploy an enterprise architecture and related practice in your organization.*"

Gerard E.A. Smit
Executive IT Architect, Computer Services Industry, IBM Technical Expert Council

---

# CONTENTS

# FOREWORD

When I was six years old, I visited an old worker and his lifetime job was to craft beautiful nails for handmade wooden doors. His theory was that a good nail head must be made with just seven blows. But, he added, "There is no good worker without good tools." His words made such an impression that I've never forgotten them.

Enterprise architecture is still a young discipline; the most advanced enterprises and professionals still have less than 10 years of experience in it. Firms still need to make various compromises when building a "good-enough" architecture within their organization – i.e., one that does not cost too much nor delays project delivery, but maintains a manageable level of coherency and complexity despite organizational (or political) complexities. A survey published in 2006 reveals that 53% of EA stakeholders see EA documentation as hard to find and use, 42% think the documentation is not specific enough, and 34% believe that EA is not involved with the business.

Starting a new architecture initiative in an enterprise that does not have it or enhancing current EA practices that can't satisfy new objectives remains a challenge. Firms can make improvements in many ways; choosing the right combination of improvements is difficult.

One of the best practices collected from Forrester's EA group research is that bringing coherency to EA requires aligning three dimensions: organization, objectives, and EA scope. Bringing coherency involves a progressive approach of better understanding and sharing EA knowledge – not just within the EA group, but also with EA stakeholders like business relationship managers, operation and development groups, the CIO, and even IT procurement in some organizations.

This book provides a number of the "good tools" that will help architects make the right choice, demonstrate why these are the right choices, and find the right progression path. They will thus become the "good" – or at least a better – enterprise architect than the one without these tools, recognizing of course, that our architects are knowledge workers rather than manual ones! This book mainly describes the use of four tools and provides numerous tips and examples:

- The first of these EA tools is the DYA architecture framework. An EA framework is a graphical, abstract representation of EA content, such as the different models, a breakdown of the details, and sometimes the viewpoints. Enterprise architecture frameworks are well-known among architects: 55% use their own custom frameworks and a further 30% use Zachman. There are more than 20 EA frameworks available on the market, ranging from extremely simple to highly complex. Choosing a framework is a best practice that enables architects to represent elements like their EA coverage and the boundaries of the responsibilities they share with business units, and to illustrate their progress with simple indicators like red lights.

- The second EA tool described here is the SWOT Analysis Process, based on a survey of EA users. Architects often work in two ways: as firemen or as policemen. A good architect is continuously alternating between these roles and adding yet others, like insurer. He must find the right balance between thought and action, but just how to go about this is often difficult to establish. The SWOT Analysis Process is a unique tool because it assesses the view of those using the architecture and provides recommendations on how to move in the right direction and find a better balance between the fireman and policeman roles.

- The third of the EA tools proposed is the Architecture Maturity Matrix. This helps prioritize where you should put the emphasis, as it is impossible to do everything at once. The use of this relatively new type of EA tool – often called enterprise architecture assessments – is not yet a best practice, as a recent survey showed us. Currently, they are used mainly by the most advanced organizations, with many using them repeatedly to assess their next steps – thus demonstrating their value. As a result, this is the tool that most organizations should adopt next.

- Finally and most importantly – and what really makes the difference in the market – is the description of a methodology with examples. Even if these different tools can be used individually, the methodology links these different tools in a framework. It helps architects create their own irreplaceable experience of correctly using the tools by giving the reader some of the important "know-how", including how to tailor these tools to obtain a better nail – sorry, a better enterprise architecture! – for your enterprise.

There are a number of other tools in this book beyond those I've included in this foreword, but it would be far better for you to discover these by actually reading the book. The appearance and developing usage of these tools and best practices demonstrate that the enterprise architect role is maturing. I hope that reading this book will make you a better-armed enterprise architect, with a wide range of good tools at your disposal.

Henry Peyret
Senior Analyst at Forrester Research
Forrester Leadership Board EA Council

# PREFACE

In recent years, we have helped many organizations to work effectively with architecture. We have seen that adopting architectural practices takes effort, and can have any number of pitfalls. Yet the DYA Model offers a stable foundation on which to build. DYA, which stands for Dynamic Architecture, provides organizations with an effective way of dealing with architecture. We outlined the basis of DYA in a book originally published in Dutch in 2001, *DYA® : snelheid en samenhang in business- en ICT-architectuur*, revised and reissued in English in 2005 as *Dynamic Enterprise Architecture: How to Make It Work*. Since that original publication, DYA has been used successfully in a variety of organizations. In this new book we share the experiences and insights that we have gained. We hope that these insights will help you to enhance the professionalism and effectiveness of your organization's architectural practices.

The present book is a practical handbook. It contains many examples from our own experiences. These examples have been reviewed by an advisory board made up of fellow experts and professionals, who discussed previous drafts of this work at regular meetings in Kasteel Montfoort. We are extremely grateful to Stella van Dijk (Police), Dick Groeneveld (Netherlands Ministry of Justice), Frank Howldar (ING), Joop Jansen (Vitens), Marten Kramer (Fortis), Siem Lakeman (ABN AMRO), Peter van der Linden (Eneco), John Mulders (Netherlands Tax and Customs Administration), Olav Ruizendaal (Interpolis), Jan Truijens (Rabobank), Edi Vermaas (SNS Bank), Bert de Wals (ING), Marcel Wijnhorst (KPN), Erwin Winkel (BAT) and Hans Zwitzer (KLM). The Montfoort sessions were enormously inspiring to us.

In addition, we would like to thank Math Dicker (Open University in the Netherlands), Rogier Dijk (Rabobank), Bert Grootjans (Achmea), Henk Koning (freelance computer scientist) and Peter Odenhoven (Hogeschool van Amsterdam) for their extensive commentaries on our manuscript.

Several colleagues from our own organization, Sogeti Nederland BV, have also contributed to the production of this book. Careful and considered readings were provided by Rien Berkhout, Pieter van Binsbergen, David van Dijk, Gerard van Eerdt, Hans Fugers, Jan Hoogervorst, Roelf Houwing, Bart Krijgsman, Joost Luijpers, Bert Nederveen, Johan Nelis, Bert Noorman, Ivo van Ouwerkerk, Allan Reid, Ria van Rijn, Martin van Run, Joep Sars, Gé Schellen, Ron

Sintemaartensdijk, Daniël Smits and Ruud Zwiers. Thanks for all your comments and suggestions. We also want to thank Erik Kieboom and Stefan Langerveld for their contributions on "thinking about change in five different colors."

We would like to thank three of our colleagues in particular: Klaas Brongers, in his own engaging manner, helped us with the publication of this book; Jack van der Linde was the perfect host and chairman for the advisory board; and Jeroen Versteeg made it possible for us to write this book. Thanks for all your assistance and support!

Writing this book has been a great pleasure, and we hope that you enjoy reading it as much. We also wish you a great deal of success in applying these insights to your own practices. We would be pleased to hear your observations and experiences: they can be emailed to dya@sogeti.nl.

July 2006

Martin van den Berg
Marlies van Steenbergen

# 1 INTRODUCTION

It is difficult for organizations to change. Many strategic initiatives end in failure because the required changes are viewed in isolation rather than in relation to each other. Years of uncoordinated revision and expansion of business operations and information management builds complexity. This drives up costs alarmingly, and makes business renewal increasingly difficult and time consuming. To turn this negative trend around, it is necessary to steer the many changes occurring in an organization simultaneously. More and more organizations are realizing that working with architecture is essential for achieving and maintaining effective business operations. However, recent years have shown us that implementing an architectural practice is not easy.

The notion of dynamic architecture (DYA, also known as dynamic enterprise architecture) was initially introduced in a book written in Dutch entitled *DYA® : snelheid en samenhang in business- en ICT-architectuur* and translated into English as *Dynamic Enterprise Architecture: How to Make It Work*. DYA addresses architecture in a way that is aimed at delivering real value to the organization. DYA not only involves the production of architecture but, more importantly, the embedding of architectural practices within the organization. Ultimately, it is not a matter of producing an architectural blueprint but of using such a document to implement changes and to achieve business goals. By architecture, we mean the set of principles and models that guides the design and realization of the processes, organizational structures, information, applications and technical infrastructure within an organization.

Since the publication of our first book, DYA has become a popular concept for a large number of organizations. Many organizations have chosen DYA as a standard operational and conceptual method for working with architecture. Without a doubt, DYA has something to offer to a large variety of businesses: ranging from multinational financial institutions to manufacturing companies and care organizations, as well as everything in between. In using it, each company adapts DYA to its own practices, making it suit the size and culture of the company involved. How businesses go about this, and especially what, in real life, does and does not work, is what this book intends to show you. In that sense, this book is the result of several intensive years of implementing DYA in many different organizations.

1

## 1.1  Goal

*Building an Enterprise Architecture Practice* will make it possible for you to enhance the professionalism and effectiveness of your own organization's architectural practices. You will be taught approaches, methods and tips. Using these, you can establish where you stand as an organization and identify the best way of making yourself more effective, always recognizing that the best way of managing change and implementing architecture will depend on specific circumstances.

This book will help you to pose the right questions, focus attention on the appropriate factors and take concrete actions. It will enable you to:

— better articulate the value added by architecture to your organization;

— determine the architectural requirements of your organization;

— identify the steps for improvement, enabling you to use architecture in a more powerful and effective manner;

— define the role of the architect.

## 1.2  Target Audience

This book is specifically intended for those responsible for or participating in their organization's architecture function. In particular, it will benefit CIOs, information managers, IT managers and architects, as well as business managers.

Additionally, this book is useful for those who are regularly involved in the changes occurring in their organization, such as change managers, product managers, process managers, information analysts and business analysts.

## 1.3  Structure

Our experiences in implementing DYA have shown that a number of factors are important for any structured use of architecture. First of all, it is necessary to have an architectural vision. Make the value that architecture adds to your organization readily apparent. Only then will you be able to stay on course. Such a vision clarifies what you wish to achieve in your organization in terms of its architecture, and provides an important guideline for the many choices and decisions that you must make in organizing the architecture function.

Subsequently, there are three architectural factors that need to be examined:

—   *Product.* In practice, architecture exists in many forms and involves many facets of the organization. Viewing it as a product, you focus on the question: when should you produce which type of architecture?

—   *Process.* Employing architecture does not only involve issuing appropriate architectural products; integrating architecture into the organization is at least as important. What are the best steps that you can take in order to improve the architecture function?

—   *Person.* How do you improve the performance of the person fulfilling the role of architect, and how does this role fit into your organization?

Not everything can be done at once, so it is a good idea to set priorities: what are you going to work on first, and what can be done later? You will develop this into a plan.

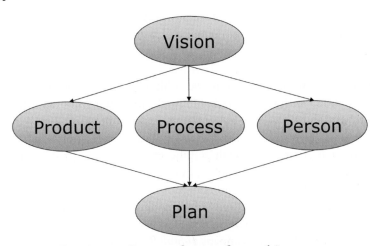

**Figure 1.1 Success factors for architecture**

These factors constitute the framework of this book and will be addressed in the various chapters.

The book begins, in Chapter 2, with the dilemmas and pitfalls involved in the employment of architecture. This chapter can be seen as the rationale for the rest of the book. It emphasizes the importance of a structured approach in working with architecture.

The development of an architectural vision is the subject of Chapter 3, a chapter that helps you clarify what you wish to achieve in your organization by adopting architectural practices.

Chapter 4 explores the ways of identifying the architectural artifacts to focus on: architecture considered as a product.

The *process* of incorporating architecture is discussed in two chapters. In Chapter 5, you will be given instructions on how to conduct a SWOT analysis in order to find the balance between thought and action in your organization. Should you wish to implement actual improvements based on this SWOT analysis, Chapter 6 uses the Architecture Maturity Matrix (introduced in the same chapter) to provide you with the means.

Besides considering architectural content and the process of dealing with architecture, there is still a third important factor: the *person*, which is to say the architect him- or herself. The activities comprising this person's role are the subject of Chapter 7.

In Chapter 8, everything is brought together into a *plan*. Which architectures do you require? Where are your strengths and weaknesses insofar as architectural practices are concerned? And what role will the architect play? All these questions are integrated into a strategy for change and action plans based on that strategy. Choosing a realistic level of ambition and exercising expectation management are important additional elements.

The book concludes, in Chapter 9, with a review of the most important points.

More detailed information about two subjects is included in the appendices: Appendix 1 contains further details of the Architecture Maturity Matrix and Appendix 2 examines "thinking about change in five different colors".

*Building an Enterprise Architecture Practice* is, above all, a practical handbook. Accordingly, it is interspersed with specific examples from practice, placed in boxes to make them easily identifiable. These are all based on our own experiences and illustrate the challenges facing organizations insofar as the development and refinement of architectural practice is concerned. Additionally, they present some solutions chosen in specific circumstances.

We introduce the fictional company *B-Sure Bank* in Chapter 2. B-Sure Bank is a bank insurer created out of a merger. It wants to use architecture to accomplish the synergy objectives that motivated the merger. The B-Sure Bank case is a recurring theme throughout the book and is used to illustrate the subjects and tools introduced in the chapters.

*Building an Enterprise Architecture Practice* is the sequel to *Dynamic Enterprise Architecture: How to Make It Work*. This book further elaborates the models introduced in the earlier publication, but it can be read on its own.

# 2 SUCCESS WITH ARCHITECTURE IS NOT AUTOMATIC

Implementing effective architectural practices means dealing with a number of pitfalls. It becomes even more difficult when an organization does not consider implementing architecture until the need for architectural artifacts is urgent.

## 2.1 Getting Lost in Content

"We need to select the head of this task force with great care – someone practical, with good contacts. How about Arnold Hedges? Wouldn't he fit the bill?"

The directors of B-Sure Bank are discussing the establishment of an architecture task force. One director, Peter Wilder, argued that B-Sure Bank needs architecture if it wants to accomplish its synergy objectives. The board is now considering who should head up the task force responsible for ensuring that such architecture is developed.

John Shipman suggests, "I think Arnold Hedges would be capable of doing the job. He has solid knowledge of the organization and knows how to stick to the main issues without getting distracted. By the way, I was involved with this sort of thing before, when I was at SIA. There, things didn't turn out so well. We asked a fellow named Richard Stellar to set up an architecture department and to draft a blueprint showing where the organization should be heading. After five months of silence, we were suddenly served with a 200-page report. It was unreadable! I tried my best but just couldn't get through it. It contained enormously detailed descriptions of processes and data, with an entire system landscape broken down into components. This enhanced flexibility, Stellar claimed. He had also mapped out a complete project schedule showing how it would all be accomplished. To top it off, he asked for 75 million dollars to undertake the entire project. Although things were going relatively well at SIA, this was crazy. He was asking us to invest 75 million dollars in something that we didn't understand. As a result, the entire document was quickly brushed aside. Stellar was, of course, enormously upset. He and two fellow employees had worked extremely hard. But he didn't understand that we had only wanted a sketch to see where we were headed with our systems –

at most a couple of sheets of paper! But a book-length report, and then to ask all of a sudden for 75 million? I hope that doesn't happen here. Have you seen any of Hedges' reports? How big are they in general?"

## 2.2  The Pitfalls

The fictional case of B-Sure Bank illustrates one of the pitfalls in architectural practice: becoming entirely submerged in the architectural content and losing sight of its purpose for the intended user. Unfortunately, this occurs frequently in real life: elegant paperwork is generated, but its content does not garner any support, the document having been produced in isolation.

A financial institution initiates a large IT program in order to replace all of its core applications with a new modular system. Once the first modules of the new system are built, the need for architecture becomes evident. An external project leader is hired and, along with two of the company's own personnel, is assigned the task of creating a logical-application architecture to better demarcate the modules in the new system. Involving the organization in creating the architecture is, for the time being, not thought necessary – after all, the two company insiders have substantial knowledge of the business and the current applications. Energy is poured into developing the architecture and, after four months, a solid product is delivered. However, it turns out that during those four months the company had been modifying its business strategy for the future. The IT program is terminated and the architecture shelved, despite the fact that the architecture provides an outstanding view of the business processes, data and functions of the current organization. The two company employees become so frustrated that they leave the organization.

This example illustrates that successfully embedding architecture within an organization involves more than just generating a product. Because the architects became so involved in the development of the architecture, they failed to realize that the organization was taking a different course. The developed architecture could still prove useful despite the turnaround in strategy, as it provides a good way of conceptualizing existing processes, data and functions. These are not yet obsolete. Yet creating the architecture in isolation means that it is not alive to the organization. This is a costly example of out of sight, out of mind.

A second pitfall is being too ambitious. Frequently, the organization wants too much all at once. It is simply impossible to establish completely professional architectural practices within a month. All kinds of things are involved, and not everything can happen simultaneously.

A third pitfall is insufficient consideration of feasibility within the organization. Every organization is different insofar as size and culture are concerned, which has consequences for architectural practices.

Finally, the architecture developed is often not relevant to the changes currently happening in the organization. For example, an architecture is developed and approved by management, then it is decreed that everyone must henceforth comply with the architecture. But the first project to come along reveals that:

—  The architecture sets conditions without indicating how the project can, in practice, meet these conditions.

—  Certain conditions of the architecture prove to be entirely impractical.

—  The architecture prohibits certain old practices, while the proposed new working procedures require an enormous amount of extra effort.

—  The architecture depends upon standard middleware that will not be in place for a few months.

Further consultation between the project manager and the sponsor determines that the project cannot comply with the architecture without increasing the duration of the project by 50 percent. And before they have had a chance to realize what is happening, the architecture team is shoved off to the periphery of the organization; they are identified as professional deadweights – certainly very intelligent individuals, but totally cut off from everyday practice. And the architecture is allowed to die.

Working with architecture clearly requires more than just drafting a document. It is a manner of working in which changes in the organization are coordinated by overarching frameworks: the architecture.

## 2.3 The Dilemma

We often find that an organization only pays serious attention to architectural practices when the need for architectural products is urgent. A situation then arises in which the designated architects are confronted by a double challenge: they must promptly deliver the architectural artifacts that the organization urgently requires; at the same time, they must implement architectural practices from scratch. They have not yet a professional environment in which to develop architectures and incorporate them into the organization.

It is a dilemma that we have to live with. We need to pay attention to generating architecture as well as to implementing the necessary practices. We must also recognize that although these are two sides of the same coin, each has its own dynamics and restrictions, and they must be dealt with differently.

Developing powerful and effective architectural practices is a process of professionalization that can extend over a period of one or two years. Throughout this time, working procedures are raised to higher levels every quarter. The production of architectural artifacts cannot be planned far in advance; it responds to immediate needs and changes that are pressing at any given moment. The production of artifacts will happen with increasing ease the higher the level of maturity on the process side.

A similar dilemma exists in organizations that have already been employing architecture for some time. These organizations have a professional environment to foster the quick provision of architectures, and a number of architectural products are available. However, the organization accepts these products only with great difficulty. The architects, for their part, are unwilling to deal with these problems of organizational buy-in. In their eyes, their primary concern is with content production. But even organizations long accustomed to working with architecture have to give due attention to both the production of architectural artifacts and the professionalization of architectural practices.

Two employees are hired as IT architects by the IT manager of a service organization. The two architects are knowledgeable with regard to the organization, the applications and the infrastructure. The IT manager wants the architects to participate directly in large projects and to orchestrate the design choices being made. Additionally, the IT manager requires an effective architecture for the entire organization.

The architects do what they can but run up against the problem that their role in the organization is unclear. Their efforts are questioned, and they find it difficult to identify the value that they add. All their energy is spent on positioning themselves. The IT manager is not sympathetic and expects them to simply get on with it. This combination of a high level of ambition and a large degree of uncertainty about the role of the architect is a self-perpetuating problem. The expectations of the IT manager, which are already high, cannot be achieved because the architects spend so much of their time explaining their own role. The IT manager becomes progressively more impatient and dissatisfied. He does not see results produced by the IT architects. The architects, meanwhile, feel that they are not being taken seriously, and they are not inspired to take initiative.

This example clearly illustrates the integration between content and process. It is critical to appreciate that work needs to be done on both in order to successfully employ architecture.

Numerous organizations face the dilemma described above, as architectural practices are gradually becoming quite common in various sectors. Underlying this evolution is the promise of integrating the changes occurring throughout the organization and discernibly strengthening their contributions to the organization's mission and objectives. Architecture offers the frameworks and guidelines required to make this happen. But the greater control and integration of change as promised by architecture does not depend solely on the quality of its content. At least as important is the degree to which architectural thinking is adopted by those who initiate and execute these changes, such as sponsors, business managers, IT managers, project managers, information analysts, designers, builders and administrators.

Architecture is used to coordinate the content of change occurring in an organization; it channels change. If nothing has to be changed, there is no need for architecture. The employment of architecture can be understood as the implementation of changes within certain contextual guidelines. Architecture can therefore only realize its promise in relation to an organization's processes of change. To use architecture as an instrument to steer change, it must be embedded into the relevant change processes. If this occurs, the chances of falling into one of the pitfalls discussed earlier will decrease substantially.

## 2.4 Architectural Practice with DYA

Working with architecture evidently involves more than just drafting an architectural blueprint. Architecture only becomes meaningful when it is related to other processes in the organization. This is illustrated by the DYA Model in Figure 2.1 (for a detailed discussion of the DYA Model, please refer to Wagter *et al.* [25]).

The core of the DYA Model consists of four processes covering the entire process of change, from strategy formation to realization:

— *Strategic Dialogue*, through which the business goals are established and elaborated by means of business cases into concrete project proposals;

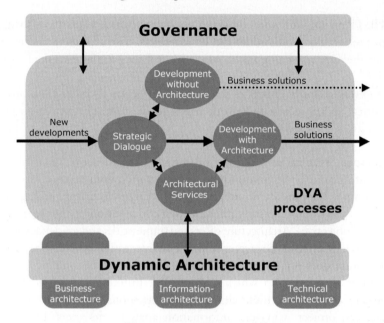

*Figure 2.1* **DYA model**

— *Architectural Services*, the processes in which the architectures are formulated and then made available to the Strategic Dialogue and Development with Architecture;

— *Development with Architecture*, in which the business goals are accomplished within the stipulated time frames and in accordance with the anticipated quality and costs – in the DYA process, Development with Architecture is the standard; and

— *Development without Architecture*, a deliberate choice in special circumstances, perhaps involving extreme time pressure, to deviate from the architectural framework.

In this model, Architectural Services (i.e. the development and maintenance of architecture) clearly constitute a support process. Architecture is not a goal in itself but a tool for managing the changes formulated in Strategic Dialogue and realized in Development with(out) Architecture. It aligns these changes so they best serve the business goals.

Because the DYA Model clearly identifies the factors involved in architectural practices, it has been adopted by many organizations. But how should it be adapted to best suit yours? A number of questions arise when you first decide to employ architecture in your own organization:

— What do you want to achieve by working with architecture in your organization?

— How do you divide your efforts between producing architectural products on the one hand and implementing architectural practices on the other?

— What level of ambition should you select?

— Which architectural artifacts should you consider?

— Are you going to formulate architectural principles and guidelines or will you devote your energy to developing models?

— How will you define the role of the architect?

— Who will be involved in your efforts, when, and in what ways?

— Where in the organization will you position the role of the architect?

— How will you gain support and acceptance for architectural practices?

To answer these questions, a clear architectural vision is needed, along with a realistic plan tailored to your situation. In this plan, a balance must be found between the generation of architectural products and the development of the architect's role.

# 3 VISION OF ARCHITECTURE

For many, architecture is a relatively abstract notion. Architects often have difficulty in clearly articulating its value. This typically leads to skepticism in the organization, causing the architects to doubt if they are, in fact, approaching things in the right way. Even worse, they may cut themselves off from the organization and bury themselves in content. Negative reactions like these can be prevented if a clear vision of architectural practice is articulated at the start. Such an architectural vision constitutes an important guiding principle for the many decisions and choices that must be made in defining and performing the architecture function.

## 3.1 Architecture? Yes, But Why?

"Now briefly explain to me what value you add?" The question posed by Peter Bennett, manager of the property and casualty department at B-Sure Bank, still rings in Arnold Hedges's ears. Arnold and Peter had just entered the elevator together and Arnold had said that he was extremely busy with the formation of an architecture task force. Arnold knew that once the doors opened they would go their separate ways, and Peter's overflowing calendar would make further discussion unlikely. For Arnold, now was his chance to make it clear to Peter, a notorious opponent of centralized frameworks, that architecture made solid sense for B-Sure Bank.

Arnold proceeded, "If we did not exist, B-Sure Bank would in time become completely bogged down. Its business operations, information flows and IT would grind to a halt." "Yes," said Peter, "that's what everyone says. But what specifically is your role in preventing this threat?"

Arnold felt that Peter was challenging him personally. It sounded as if his job were on the line. He made a second attempt: "My group and I make sure that this organization remains cohesive. B-Sure Bank consists of a conglomeration of islands. I build the bridges between these islands so that we can face the world as a united country." Arnold was satisfied; that came out short and sweet.

The elevator stopped at the eleventh floor, where Peter got off. Before he left, he turned to Arnold and said, "It's still not entirely clear to me. In any case, you're certainly passionate about it and that means something. Make an appointment with my secretary and we'll speak more on the subject."

Pleased about this opening, Arnold strolled to his workstation. He was going to make an appointment with Peter immediately, and to prepare for their meeting he would become absolutely clear about what architecture meant to B-Sure Bank.

## 3.2 An Architectural Vision Provides Steady Footing

The situation at B-Sure Bank is typical of the practices involving enterprise, information and IT architecture throughout the world. Companies are extremely preoccupied with architecture but cannot always quite say why. Architectural initiatives are often introduced to meet a need for more control over organizational development or in response to some inkling about more efficient or effective operations. In most cases, the people directly involved have their own personal view of the importance of architecture and its added value for the organization. Yet something more is required to communicate this clearly to outsiders. Too often, such communication involves nothing more than vague notions about providing cohesion, harmonizing developments or preparing for the future. All true, but too abstract to be effective in showing people the usefulness of architecture.

In a large organization, one that could not conceivably do without architecture – or so you might think – around 25 architects, spread throughout business units and the IT department, have been kept busy with architecture for years. Assemble these architects together in a workshop, and they are all clearly of the opinion that their contribution is obvious. In fact, it is unthinkable that this organization could operate without architecture. Ask them to take part in a role play involving a so-called elevator pitch (i.e. explain the added value of the architecture department to a member of higher management in the time it takes an elevator to arrive at the eleventh floor), and they find it extremely difficult to do. When the CIO later makes his appearance at the workshop, the exercise turns out to be extremely pertinent. The CIO announces that large cutbacks are being made and that one should not be surprised if, in the short term, the extent and even existence of the architecture function were subject to discussion.

Obviously, architecture is important for this large organization. It seems inconceivable that the organization could operate without it. But why is it so difficult to explain this importance in a clear and transparent manner?

Architecture and its development is relatively far removed from the primary business processes of an organization. It does not, for example, have any direct impact on such processes as marketing services or manufacturing products. Its influence is less direct. Architectural practices ensure that revisions to business processes, information flows and technical structure, revisions necessitated by changing requirements inside and outside the organization, are implemented in a coherent manner. The importance of this coherence is, however, not always evident. After all, we can also make changes without architecture. Therefore it is extremely important to be able to clearly explain the value added by employing architecture.

One way of explaining the value added by architecture involves the formulation of an architectural vision, which should then be recorded in a vision document. This vision is a strategy, a starting point for all architectural initiatives and a tool to keep the architects on course. Clarifying the contribution expected from architecture provides a focus for the architect and reduces the chance that he or she will get lost in content. Moreover, it provides security and confirmation: you know why you are doing it. In addition, a clear architectural vision provides a consistent basis for communication. It can be used as a constant reference point in presentations, newsletters and publications. The consistency reinforces the organization's confidence in the architecture function.

## 3.3  The Why, What and How of Architecture

Figure 3.1 indicates the most important issues involved in an architectural vision. Why are we implementing architecture? What do we understand architecture to include? How does architecture benefit the organization? And how will we define the architecture function?

The decision to employ architecture does not generally fall from the sky. There is a reason behind it, and that reason can vary. It may stem from a new manager who is convinced that "things could be better" to an organizational crisis originating inside or outside the organization. This motivation is mostly a good indication of the purpose that must be achieved by architecture, but it should not be confused with that purpose. The immediate motivation is often a symptom, while the purpose is the underlying problem that needs to be addressed. For instance, the apparent motivation for using architecture can be the fact that harmony between two projects threatens to go awry. However, the ultimate purpose involves the desire to use architecture to better manage the project portfolio.

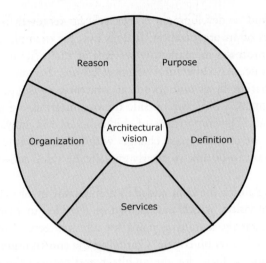

***Figure 3.1* Elements of an architectural vision**

Even though the apparent reason for using architecture may not directly address the underlying problem, it is advisable to compose the architectural vision with the apparent reason in mind. The apparent problem is a pain that needs to be treated and, in future, prevented. The architectural vision aims to cure the pain. If the organization threatens to fall back into its old habits, it is useful to recall this pain-avoidance motive: "Remember why we began to use architecture …"

If the purpose of architectural practices underlying the apparent reason for adopting them is also clear, this purpose provides an important guideline for all the decisions and activities in the architectural domain. Clarifying the purpose is not only important to justify the investment in people and resources, but it helps to determine the elements that need to be emphasized. After all, architecture comes in various manifestations and forms. Where should we begin? Which forms should we choose? Who will have to work with them? All these questions depend upon, among other things, the purpose that we want the architecture to serve. Examples of purposes for adopting architectural practices are to manage a best-of-breed policy, to support project-portfolio management, or to identify and realize opportunities for synergy and the breaking down of barriers between departments.

Two financial institutions decide to implement architectural practices. In so doing, the purpose of the first institution is to better streamline working procedures and the design choices being made in IT projects. Ultimately, a consistent mode of operation is to be adopted. In particular, recurring heated discussions about fundamental issues need to be limited and, ultimately, resolved. With this purpose in mind, it is decided to primarily focus on drafting general principles and policy guidelines in the area of information and technical architecture.

The second institution considers the primary purpose of its architecture to be maintaining coherence throughout the various strategic business projects that have recently been initiated. The most important concern is that the business decisions made in the context of the projects intermesh and fit into an overarching vision and strategy. As a consequence, they decide to establish a business model as quickly as possible, one that will provide a framework for positioning and controlling all the ongoing projects.

Depending on its purpose, the architecture will have a different focus, both in terms of its content (is it primarily centered on IT or business?) and its f (does it mostly involve guidelines or models?).

If the purpose of the architecture is not equally clear to everyone, or if the various people involved have different objectives in mind, expectations may diverge. If this happens, support and approval for architectural practices may disappear.

In a pension company, architecture is viewed by the IT department as a means of arriving at a market-determined level of costs. The company's business units regard architecture as a means of achieving better alignment between business developments and IT. Because these stakeholders do not clearly express their expectations to each other, a great deal of misunderstanding and misconception about architecture results.

Keeping the purpose of architecture clearly in the minds of all the stakeholders provides clarity from which everyone will profit. For one thing, the reason for all the investment and effort can be communicated in an unequivocal and powerful manner. Practice teaches us that the question of "why" recurs often. This question must be answered consistently throughout the organization for there to be confidence in the architecture. Additionally, a clear purpose establishes a foundation upon which to develop architecture, and provides a framework for testing decisions about the architectural principles and choices. Also, because it is impossible to do everything at once, a clear sense of purpose helps to prioritize tasks. Finally, awareness of purpose can be used to constantly monitor how and to what degree the architecture is adopted in practice. Drafting elegant architectural documents does not, after all, automatically achieve the stated purpose. More is needed: the architecture must give rise to appropriate changes in the organization. The effectiveness of the architectural processes can also be tested in this way.

Besides the *why* of architecture (the purpose), the *what* is also important: the third element of the architectural vision. By defining architecture, an organization can express what it understands as architecture, which parts of it are to be adopted and in which form architecture is to be used.

There are many definitions of architecture created by those in the field, such as IEEE 1471, IAF and of course DYA. The question is not which one is right but which is most usable for a specific organization. In each case, an organization must judge what it wants to achieve with the architecture and which definition is most suitable for that purpose.

### IEEE 1471

The definition of IEEE 1471-2000 [7] is widely accepted as the basis of architecture: "the fundamental organization of a system embodied in its components, their relationships to each other and to the environment, and the principles guiding its design and evolution."

### IAF

Rijsenbrij *et al.* [20] define architecture as "a coherent, consistent collection of principles, differentiated into basic assumptions, rules, guidelines and standards (sometimes forming patterns), that describe how an enterprise, information flow, information system or infrastructure is designed and appears in use."

### DYA

Wagter *et al.* [25] use the following definition for architecture: "the consistent set of rules and models that guides the design and implementation of processes, organizational structures, information, applications and the technical infrastructure within an organization."

Any given organization, in choosing a definition, should indicate as concretely as possible the nature and the scope of the architecture. If the architecture is limited to IT, say so in the definition. If the architecture merely involves the drafting of principles and standards to guide design, identify those items – and nothing more.

An international industrial group in the field of food items and luxury foods has a production facility in the Netherlands. This facility is experiencing an increasing need for integration. Externally, it needs better alignment in a supply chain involving various countries and marketing organizations. Internally, ERP systems need to be synchronized with production management systems. This is the reason why architectural practices are introduced. The scope of the architecture encompasses all of the IT systems (the administrative and logistical systems) and the manufacturing systems. Since the environment of the production facility is in constant flux, the process of actualizing and managing the architecture is of great importance. One of the demands placed on the architecture is that it must be understandable. The culture of the company is characterized as "not words but deeds." Taking stock of all this, the following definition of architecture is chosen:

— A comprehensive set of principles for both the parent company and the production facility, as well as choices in the areas of IT and manufacturing systems.

— In addition, the process of arriving at these choices and properly recording them.

In effect, this chosen definition better suits the organization and is more readily accepted by it than a conceptual, possibly more water-tight but also more abstract formulation derived from the literature.

For the employees of an organization, it is often unclear what architects do. The construction of a sort of service catalogue, the fourth component of the architectural vision, is a manner of clarifying what the organization may expect from the architects. After all, the customer is the starting point for any service description. Which of the customer's problems can be resolved by which service? Taking the customer's point of view has an added advantage: it allows the customer benefits of architecture to be explicitly detailed.

The Architecture and Advice department (A&A), a subdivision of the IT department at a mid-sized financial institution, has produced a service catalogue that distinguishes between services for business units and services for its own IT department.

For the business units, A&A provides support in aligning business needs with the possibilities of IT. Support is offered for:

- aligning needs and possibilities (business-IT alignment)

- issuing proposals for new developments in the field of IT

- drafting information plans

- formulating business cases

- investigating trends in business, technology, platforms and suppliers for the coming years

- initiating, managing and executing innovative projects and proof-of-concepts stemming from the information plans, as well as offering guidance during implementation

- developing IT architectures for the business units

- performing IT-architecture scans (taking inventory of current IT architecture and making recommendations)

The construction of business architecture is the work and responsibility of the business units. A&A can make contributions in this regard as part of its business consultancy role.

A&A is responsible for the IT architecture within the IT department. This responsibility (inside IT) can be broken down into:

- developing IT architecture

- supporting projects in their efforts to comply with IT architecture by, among other things, fielding questions raised during the projects

- verifying compliance with IT architecture

- implementing architectural practices within the IT department

- issuing guidelines to deal with systems that do not comply with the desired architecture

- providing generic services to projects (generic services are standard components within IT development and management)

This service catalogue illustrates the limitations that the A&A department experiences because of its position in the IT department. Due to this position, it is difficult to have business units accept A&A's business architecture (products/services, processes and organization). As a consequence, A&A goes no further than offering assistance in the construction of business architecture, with the hope that the business will carry the baton further itself.

The final element of the architectural vision (in addition to its reason, purpose, definition and services) involves the organization of the architect's role. How are the architects organized? Which tasks do they take up (along with the associated roles and responsibilities)? Which processes do they perform themselves? How will they collaborate with others while performing their tasks? What role will they play in processes performed by others? And, finally, who is to formally approve the architectural choices?

A good vision document takes up about three pages. It must contain the key elements of the architectural vision. If this proves impossible, the whole affair is likely too complex. Details concerning such items as services and organization can, if necessary, be elaborated in one or more support documents.

## 3.4 Producing an Architectural Vision

Reason, purpose, definition, services and organization together constitute the vision of how an organization is employing architecture. Realizing this vision usually occurs in a number of phases. In general, the person responsible for the architecture will form an impression of the desired role and outcome of the architecture function. With this scheme in mind, the architect can then turn to the organization in order to test the practicality of the vision and, in discussions with the most important stakeholders, refine it. Conversation is an important factor in forming an architectural vision. What can be said about architecture itself can also be said about the vision of architecture: the means of getting there is at least as important as the end result.

Organizations that have not yet developed anything in the way of architecture must begin at the beginning: by increasing the awareness of what architecture can mean for the organization. A workshop is a suitable forum in which to generate this increased awareness because it brings several people from different disciplines together. In planning the workshop, consider involving IT and business management. A possible scenario for such a workshop is reproduced in Table 3.1.

*Table 3.1* **Scenario for an architecture awareness workshop**

| Section | Result |
| --- | --- |
| *Purpose and program workshop* | General themes for the day |
| *Architecture new?* | |
| Make an inventory, in an interactive manner, of what the organization already possesses in terms of architecture: | Foster awareness of what architecture is and the fact that the organization already possesses architecture, if not under that name. |
|   — What are the main requirements that the organization imposes on products/services, processes, organization, information flows and IT? | |
|   — What are the most important standards and guidelines? | |
|   — What policy documents exist? | |
| *Introduction to architecture* | |
| By means of a presentation, provide information about what architecture is, the added value that it can furnish and the implications of architectural practice. Use many examples in order to make architecture as vivid as possible to the participants. | Draft a theoretical and practical framework to further assist the participants to position architecture in their own organization. |
| *Use of architecture* | |
| By means of a current issue in the organization, investigate how architecture might contribute to solving the issue. | Raise awareness that architecture helps unravel complex issues and clarify coherence. |
| *Importance of architecture* | |
| Conduct a discussion on the possible importance of architecture in the participants' organization. | Deliver a first impression of what architecture could mean for the participants' organization. |
| *Closing and conclusion* | |
| Discuss outstanding issues and arrive at agreements. | Come to agreements about the future. |

The contribution of architecture to the business goals of the organization may be more clearly expressed using what is called *benefit logic*. Benefit logic establishes a relation between the strategic goals of the organization and architectural practice. The mission, vision and strategy of an organization contain identifiable strategic goals, such as a certain return on invested capital. The question then raised concerns the manner in which the employment of architecture contributes to achieving this return.

**Figure 3.2** **Basis of benefit logic**

This is not a direct relationship but one that proceeds along a number of channels. By revealing these channels, the added value of architectural practice becomes clear, as demonstrated in Figure 3.3.

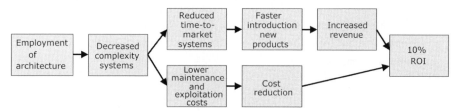

**Figure 3.3** **Full benefit logic**

Of course, the implementation of architecture is not the only factor that affects an organization's profits. But in the manner demonstrated, it certainly becomes clear how the use of architecture is one of the contributing factors. This type of diagram is also a powerful communications tool. Benefit logic can also be used by management to test the effectiveness of architecture.

The communication of the *what* and *why* of architecture has proven to be difficult in practice. Every architect finds that conveying the message in a concise and convincing manner is not easy. An architecture communication workshop has proven to be a useful tool in clarifying the *what* and *why* of architecture. In various role plays, architects rehearse explanations of the architectural *what*s and *why*s. Identifying the most appealing statements made in each scenario provides elements that can be used to refine notions about architectural practice.

The additional advantage of an architecture communication workshop is that architects formulate and rehearse messages directed at various target groups, whether a presentation for a specific target audience or an informal discussion in the elevator or by the coffee machine.

In preparation for an architecture communication workshop, two architects from a care institution were given the following assignment:

"The board of directors is closely involved in an IT governance project. This project has repeatedly made recommendations addressing the organization's need for frameworks. The board of directors knows that an architectural scheme is in place but has a few questions and some objections. Everyone is talking about architecture and frameworks, but what do they mean? What are the advantages of having frameworks? What does the organization gain from them? Do they not detract from the flexibility and entrepreneurial spirit in the organization?

The board has invited you to come and, in no more than ten minutes, explain what architecture means to the organization and what it provides."

In this exercise, there are two important lessons:

(i)  above all, do not say too much; limit yourself to the core message; and

(ii) tell your story from the outside in (from the perspective of the target group) and not from the inside out (from the viewpoint of the architecture function).

## 3.5  B-Sure Bank's Architectural Vision

B-Sure Bank is an international financial services provider. The company is known as a bank insurer and is therefore active both in the banking sector and in the field of insurance. In the Netherlands, B-Sure Bank is a large player, but it is also active in other European countries and in North America.

B-Sure Bank offers its services under the names of B-Bank, Virtuality and Personality, which are all divisions of the current organization:

— B-Bank targets its investment and loan services to the business community.

— Virtuality concentrates on private individuals, providing them with such services as payment transactions, savings, investments, loans and mortgages. The primary service vehicle is the internet.

— Personality aims at both the business community and private individuals, offering them the banking services provided by B-Bank and Virtuality, as well as insurance (property, casualty, life and health care).

Figure 3.4 displays the organizational structure.

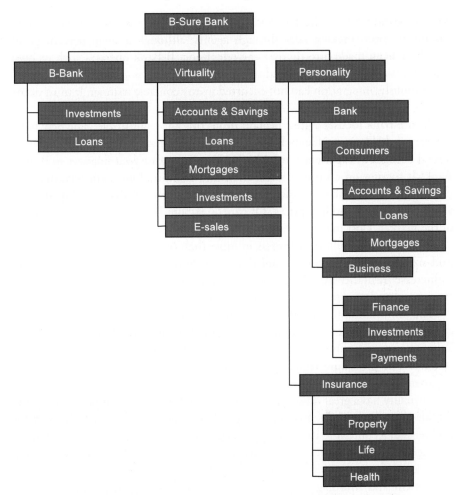

***Figure 3.4* Organizational structure of B-Sure Bank**

B-Sure Bank was recently created by the merger of the Personality Group and the former business bank known as B-Bank. Although both parties complement each other well, there is a clear overlap in the services being provided. Further integration of the businesses is planned. This integration must, on the one hand, lead to a more efficient use of resources while, on the other hand, increasing sales of insurance products in particular. As a result of the merger, Personality also gained access to the B-Bank subsidiary, Virtuality. Virtuality is the best-known financial service provider on the internet. Its acquisition offers Personality the opportunity to move from its trailing position in internet banking into a leading position within a very short period of time. The insurance arm of Personality has mostly been making sales through agents, although a small percentage of sales have been made directly over the telephone. B-Bank operates with its own consultants and has offices around the world.

Previously, integration had not occurred in any concrete manner. It must occur now.

B-Sure Bank focuses a great deal on projecting the right image. The new bank insurer would like to profile itself as a reliable, expert financial service provider with several decades of experience: it is absolutely safe to trust your finances to B-Sure Bank. It focuses on customer satisfaction and building long-term relationships: choosing B-Sure Bank is a choice for life. Consequently, reliability and quality are valued over speed and low prices. Of course, B-Sure Bank cannot price itself out of the market. Cost management is certainly a consideration.

With over ten million customers in more than 60 countries, B-Sure Bank is a mid-sized bank insurer on the global stage. B-Sure Bank's growth objectives are to increase insurance sales by 20 percent within two years (especially to existing customers) and to expand its customer base by 15 percent.

The information flows within the divisions of B-Sure Bank have become more complex over the years. Customer data is stored in all types of different systems. When a customer submits a change of address, it has to be processed by various systems. The procedure regularly results in errors. Each division has its own IT department.

Virtuality has a great diversity of systems. The E-sales department (responsible for sales over the internet) has, for example, Sun-Solaris servers and NT servers for the website, a content management package, a security package, a personalization package and an application for registering users. Using MQSeries, customer data is retrieved from the databases belonging to the Accounts & Savings, Loans, Investment and Mortgage departments. Each of these four departments has its own administration. The mortgage system was developed by the department's own staff using Oracle; it runs on an RS/6000. The systems for Accounts & Savings, as well as for loans, were developed using Microfocus Cobol Workbench on a HP-UX. The investment application is a SQL-Server application running on an NT server. Each department records its own customer data.

B-Bank has developed all its applications in Cobol, which runs on an IBM mainframe computer using IMS. The administration of the investment portfolios is supported by a number of standard packages.

Personality has bits and pieces of all the types of software imaginable. Over the decades, every department has built up its own system in its own environment.

Whenever interfaces are required, these are realized using one-to-one remote procedure calls.

The merger to form B-Sure Bank created significant overlap within the organization. The directors are striving to achieve synergy in these areas of overlap, and the job of the new architecture task force led by Arnold Hedges is to help achieve this synergy. Arnold's brief conversation with Peter Bennett in the elevator made him realize the importance of being able to provide a concise and convincing statement of the added value that employing architecture provides to B-Sure Bank. He decided to put his own view of his duties on paper and to test it in the organization. The result is the following first draft of a vision document.

---

**Architecture at B-Sure Bank**

*Introduction*
The goal of this document is to indicate the objectives that B-Sure Bank wishes to achieve in working with architecture and the ways in which the architectural function at B-Sure Bank is to be defined.

This document is intended as an internal communication paper for B-Sure Bank. It is meant to channel the discussion concerning architecture. Based on responses to this document, the draft will be revised and further refined. In this sense, it is a document in development.

*1 Why architecture?*
The immediate reason for implementing architecture at B-Sure Bank is the need for synergy. Due to the recent merger of the Personality Group with B-Bank, quite a lot of overlap has been created in our organization, in areas involving products and services, processes, systems and infrastructure. By employing architecture, we anticipate not only being able to identify the possibilities for synergy but actually utilizing them.

In the coming two years, the desired synergy must result in the achievement of the following objectives:

— 20 percent more sales;

— expansion of the customer base by 15 percent.

The increased sales must primarily come from existing customers. This means that we must seek out possibilities for cross-selling, in which existing customers acquire other products from us. For this purpose, the business has to gain better insight into customer behavior and sales per product/market combination. The

---

current information flow is insufficient in this regard: there is a large overlap in the systems gathering the information, yet the interrelationships among the data in these systems is unclear, so it is impossible to obtain a clear view of customers and sales. Architecture must make changes in this regard by distinguishing clear domains for both products and customer groups, and by facilitating effective data management for each domain.

B-Sure Bank would like to increase its customer base by using new technology to expand its services and distribution channels. Accordingly, the support systems will need to be updated promptly, although the current overlap of functionality inhibits this. Additionally, a number of systems are greatly out of date, and updating will be a complicated and lengthy task. For these reasons there must be a reorganization and/or modernization, where architecture will set the course. All of this is represented in the figure below.

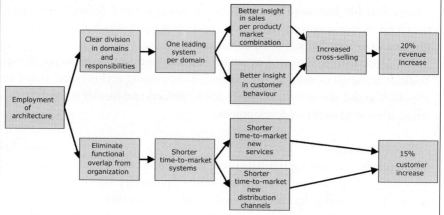

*Figure 3.5* **Benefit logic for B-Sure Bank**

In conclusion, B-Sure Bank has a clear purpose for adopting architecture: *To provide a new order of services, processes, data and systems by means of which B-Sure Bank's growth objectives can be achieved in an efficient manner.*

By restructuring services, processes, data and systems, redundancy can be eliminated and the entire information supply simplified, thereby achieving synergy.

The purpose defined above is the basis for an architecture that involves the following:

— division of B-Sure Bank into business domains;

— models for the services, processes, data and systems in each business domain, which fall under the responsibility of that domain;

— guidelines covering the design and implementation of services, processes, data and systems.

## 2 *Performing the architecture function*

At present, the architecture function at B-Sure Bank is being performed by the architecture task force. This task force is a team of six architects from various divisions of B-Sure Bank under the leadership of A.P. Hedges. The task force reports directly to the board of directors.

The primary responsibilities of the task force are developing and maintaining the architecture at B-Sure Bank and advising on the migration process. These duties involve the identification of business domains (based upon which services, processes, data and systems will be reorganized) and the subsequent mapping of the current situation to the new order. The architecture will be developed in intensive collaboration with all the stakeholders at B-Sure Bank and submitted to the board of directors for formal approval.

Additionally, the task force provides the following services for the various divisions at B-Sure Bank:

— consultation about issues in business restructuring related to scope and method;

— support for the redevelopment of processes and systems;

— (assistance for the) formulation of business cases;

— drafting and delivery of appropriate principles and models at the commencement of programs and projects;

— advice to directors about the desirability and feasibility of planned programs and projects.

The task force places specific emphasis on business activities: the provision of good support in order to arrive at the appropriate services and processes. Data and systems are then based upon these business activities. The actual IT domain (platforms, databases and infrastructure) is, for the time being, placed outside the scope of the architectural responsibilities.

# 4 EFFECTIVE ARCHITECTURE

Working with architecture means governing changes in the organization by means of organization-wide direction setting models and principles (i.e. the architecture). It is impossible to set up such a framework for all the facets of an organization. Consequently, choices must be made concerning content, scope, depth and form of the architecture.

## 4.1 A Veritable Hodgepodge

"Help! What a mishmash of architecture you have." Anne Moreland let the words slip before she could check that thought.

Kevin McAndrew glanced up. He was filling her in on the architectures at B-Sure Bank.

Kevin was a member of the architecture task force and had been asked by Arnold Hedges if he would show Anne Moreland what the architecture at B-Sure Bank was all about. Anne had been working at Telebel for years but was now ready for a new challenge – which she expected to find at B-Sure Bank. After all, B-Sure Bank stood on the cusp of a number of changes. Kevin made this quite evident in his tour of the company architecture. Anne had read the vision document about architecture and was curious to learn how it would be further elaborated into architectural frameworks. First of all, Kevin showed her the key diagram showing the direction in which B-Sure Bank wants to move in the coming years (Figure 4.1).

When Anne asked Kevin the purpose of the diagram, Kevin fell silent for a moment. "This is our new business model," he said.

Anne replied, "That's all great, but how does it relate to the vision document?"

Kevin answered, "This is the new structure for B-Sure Bank; this is where we want to get to."

"OK, I understand that," said Anne, "but how did you come up with this structure? Who thought of it? And what do you intend to do with it?"

Kevin shrugged his shoulders and unveiled the following diagram (Figure 4.2). It was one he knew all about, as he had drafted it himself.

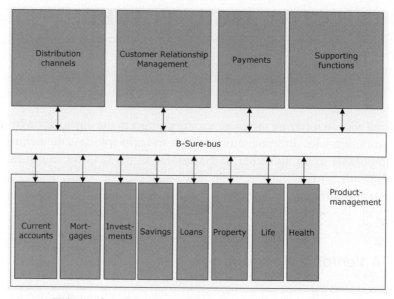

*Figure 4.1* **Future architecture at B-Sure Bank**

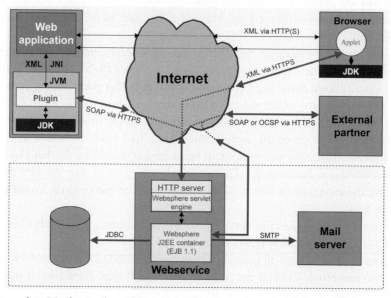

*Figure 4.2* **Technical architecture for B-Sure Bank property and casualty insurance**

"This is a new architecture for the property and casualty insurance that we would like to offer on the internet," said Kevin.

"Very concrete," replied Anne, "but how does it fit into the big picture?"

Again, Kevin could not answer. He turned to the following diagram (Figure 4.3).

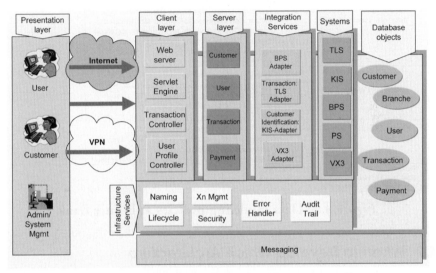

***Figure 4.3*** **System architecture for Personality**

"This figure shows how we would like to revamp the systems at Personality for use on the internet," Kevin said.

"You make very nice diagrams," remarked Anne. "Impressive! How do you check the coherence of the diagrams? And do you also provide guidelines for their interpretation?"

"We are currently busy working on that," Kevin replied, revealing a page on the intranet that contained the policies in the area of data modeling (Figure 4.4).

"OK," said Anne. "This does give me something to hold on to."

Kevin was glad to be able to provide Anne with a satisfactory response. Still, it struck him now that the architectures were extremely divers. She was right about that.

| N° | Guideline | Information | R | S | Date |
|----|-----------|-------------|---|---|------|
| 2.1 | Data is only maintained in the source file designated for this purpose. | For the sake of manageability, data is maintained at only one location, known as the source file. Other applications requiring the same data obtain it from the source file. | | A | 20-10-2004 |
| 2.2 | Data is retrieved from the distribution database designated for this purpose or, if a distribution database does not exist, from the designated source file. | To lighten the load on source files and to integrate data from various sources, distribution databases have been created. Using these databases, the data is distributed to all the applications in which it is required. If a distribution database does not (yet) exist, the data is retrieved directly from the source file. | | A | 20-10-2004 |
| 2.3 | The data clients are responsible for any necessary conversion of data into specific formats. | In effect, every application has its own format. It is not the task of the source file or the distribution database to comply with these formats. The source file or distribution database provides the data in one standard format. Client applications must undertake the necessary conversions themselves. | | A | 20-10-2004 |
| 2.4 | The data provided by a source file is not to contain any application-specific elements. | Examples of application-specific elements are internal codes and internal process data. For the sake of flexibility, it is important that these elements not be exchanged with other applications. | | A | 20-10-2004 |
| 2.5 | No meaningful coding is used. | Meaningful coding leads to unwanted dependencies and, consequently, large degrees of inflexibility. Coding is used for unique identification and not to store extra information. | | A | 20-10-2004 |

R: References to underlying documentation
S: Status (Provisional, Approved, in Revision, Outdated)
Date: Last change of status

*Figure 4.4* **Data modeling policies at B-Sure Bank**

## 4.2 When to Develop Which Architecture

The diversity of architectures in organizations is enormous, not only among organizations but often within a single organization. There are variations in depth, scope, aspect and form. A small organization can easily have cupboards full of architectural documents, all composed at some time by some individual or team somewhere in the organization for a particular purpose.

The diversity in possible architectures is reflected in the terminology employed in the technical literature, at conferences and within the organizations themselves. For example, there is business architecture, enterprise architecture, information architecture, IT architecture, infrastructure architecture, information-system architecture, domain architecture, technical architecture, process architecture, application architecture, software architecture and data architecture. The manner in which each of these types of architecture is defined varies from architect to architect.

We see organizations wrestling with this architectural multiplicity and we see the same questions popping up continuously. Which architectures does an organization require? What forms, depths and scopes must they have? And what degree of coherence should exist among them? Even if an architectural vision has been formulated for the organization and it actually indicates the ultimate purpose of architectural practice, this still does not provide any direct answer to the question which architecture is required the most. Nevertheless, the multiplicity of possibilities forces an organization to make choices. If they are not made in a careful manner, there is a great danger that, on the one hand, architecture will be created that nobody needs, while on the other hand, nothing will be provided where frameworks are actually needed.

## 4.3 From Inside Out: Variety in Architecture

In DYA, architecture is defined as a consistent set of rules and models that guides the design and implementation of processes, organizational structures, information, applications and the technical infrastructure within an organization.

Architecture can therefore be concerned with various aspects of an organization, such as products and services, processes, organizational structure, data, applications, middleware, platforms and networks. In addition, architecture can exist in various forms, including general principles, policy directives and models. This is illustrated in the DYA architectural framework (Figure 4.5).

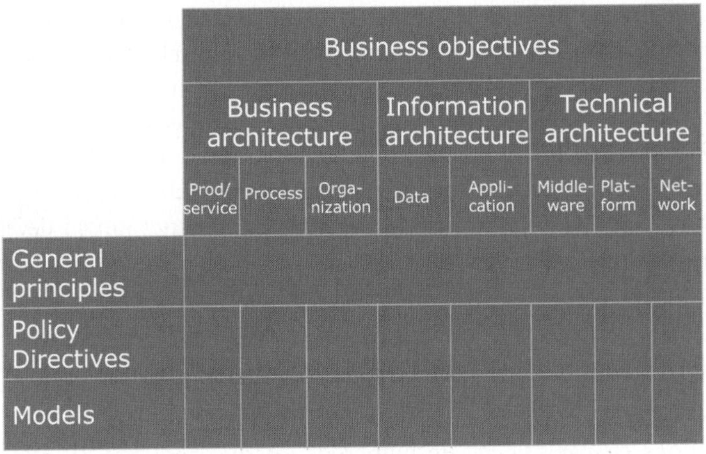

*Figure 4.5* **DYA architectural framework**

The DYA framework represents two important architectural dimensions: the aspect areas with which the architecture is concerned (the columns) and the forms that the architecture may take (the rows). But there is more. Other dimensions that, in practice, play an important role are the scope (branch of industry, enterprise or business unit) and the depth (number of distinct levels).

Consequently, there are quite a few choices to make, and the question is where to begin. There is a logical order to the framework. Insofar as the aspect areas are concerned, everything follows from the products and services that an organization delivers. Providing products or services requires processes; the execution of these processes requires an organization; data is generated and used in the processes, and they are supported by applications; these applications run on middleware, on specific platforms, and everything is connected by a network.

Logically, we begin with the construction of architectures on the left of the table and work step-by-step to the right. Sounds simple, but in practice there are many snags. If this approach is carried out in a thorough manner, the entire process will easily take a couple of years – time many organizations do not have. Furthermore, how deep does one have to go into each one of the aspects? Is it really necessary to elaborate all these factors throughout the organization? Could one set up a technical architecture without products/services? If application architecture were urgently required, would we still need to complete the four columns on the left? How fast can this all happen?

In practice, an architectural framework proves to be extremely useful in managing architectural initiatives and monitoring the coherence among architectures. In addition, it is an excellent communication tool for clarifying what precisely we mean when we are talking about architecture. But a framework is not a sufficient basis for any organizational decision about specific architectural needs or priorities, not to mention the scope, depth and form that the architectures must have. The architectural discipline cannot, by itself, supply an answer to the question, "What architecture with which characteristics must I develop, and when?" Answering such a question requires insight into business developments.

## 4.4 From Outside In: The Organizational Need

Organizations change. There are numerous internal and external triggers that prompt an organization to introduce new products onto the market, use new distribution channels, streamline processes or implement new technologies. As a rule, whenever a new idea appears to be a money-maker, the changes required to put the idea into effect will be initiated. This innovation may be part of an organization's strategy, or it may emerge *ad hoc* at any given moment. An idea results in a specific business goal, which in turn leads to change. To achieve business goals in a coherent manner, there is a need for architecture. In this way, the question about the type of architecture that is necessary at any particular time is, in fact, answered: it is fully determined by the proposed changes that the organization is to undergo. In other words, an architecture must be aligned with the organization's business goals.

If an organization is considering the possibility of introducing a new product onto the market, just enough architectural principles and models have to be defined to steer the changes required for this purpose. Does this architecture contain the same elements as the architecture in an organization wishing to convert from a product-focused to a process-focused structure? Partly yes, partly no. Likely, the same aspects (business, information, technical) are involved in both architectures. But the scope and the level of detail are different.

Depending on the magnitude of the business goal and the changes associated with it, the architecture will have a different character. Take, for example, the organization that wishes to convert from a product to a process orientation. The changes involved in such a transition affect the entire organization, so the scope of the business goal is large. The associated architecture mostly involves the ordering and clustering of organizational functions into autonomous domains, the determination of the characteristics and requirements in each domain and the recognition of the shared or infrastructural facilities interlinking them. This type of architecture is broad and at a high conceptual level. Other examples of business goals leading to an architecture of similar breadth are the structural improvement of the collaboration among parties in a supply chain, the quest for synergy between two organizations after a merger and the structural acceleration of the time-to-market for new products.

To operate more effectively, an insurance company decides to give business units more autonomy. Previously, the company has had strong central management that, over the years, has developed bureaucratic tendencies. Consequently, the time required for product introductions is beginning to grow unacceptably long. However, not everything is to be devolved to the business units. All the acquired synergy advantages, which are unquestionably sound, would then be lost. And to best serve the customer, the insurer certainly has to remain one company.

A high-level functional model is established to support the decisions to be made about decentralization. It identifies the functions to be performed centrally as well as those to be realized in each business unit:

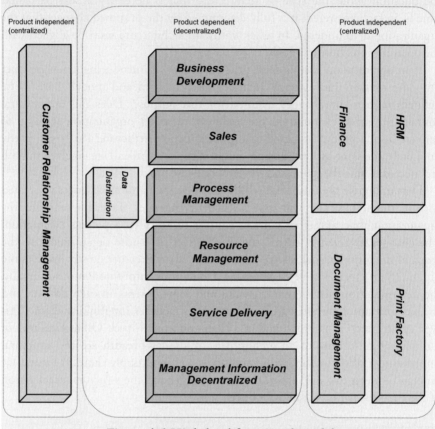

*Figure 4.6* **High-level functional model**

Not all the changes in an organization are equally far-reaching. If the business goal is to introduce a new product, it is necessary to design an architecture that directs the changes required to achieve this particular aim. In this case, architecture is needed to formulate a business case, to determine the business goal's feasibility and achievability. Such architecture describes the requirements that are imposed, the architectural principles that apply and the models that indicate how processes, data, applications and technical infrastructures must be adapted. In this case, the scope is limited to the single business unit. Other examples of business goals with a more limited scope are achieving a 50-percent acceleration of through-put time for a development process, changing the tax rate from 6 to 19 percent to comply with legal requirements, reducing the costs of a transaction from 1 to 0.10 euros, or offering a new service to examine invoices over the internet.

## 4.5 Architecture: A Question of Perspective

Business goals determine an architecture's scope and the aspects of the organization to be addressed. The intended use and target group are also critical factors: they determine the required depth and form of the architecture. This can best be illustrated with the help of the DYA Model (Figure 4.7).

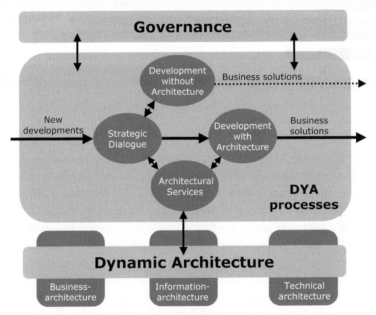

*Figure 4.7* **DYA model**

In various ways, architecture plays a role in an organization's processes of change, which are represented in the model as Strategic Dialogue and Development with(out) Architecture. Strategic Dialogue is the process of developing new ideas and creating business goals. These business goals are elaborated into business cases and project proposals. The process of Development with Architecture is concerned with actually accomplishing the business goals. In Architectural Services, architectures are formulated to support Strategic Dialogue and Development with Architecture. These are architectures that support strategic decision making, make it possible to set up business cases and provide the necessary frameworks for projects.

In most cases, the first type of architecture (intended to facilitate strategic decision making) has a coordinating function. These architectures are meant to recognize shared features, position individual developments and govern mutual coherence. They are used to channel the overall set of changes, but also to ensure that any infrastructural requirements are met on time. This form of architecture exists at a very high conceptual level, has a broad scope and serves as support for senior management in its strategic decision making. Mostly called *enterprise architecture* or, especially in large holding and multinational companies, *corporate architecture*, it is often compared to a city plan.

Architectures intended to provide support at the tactical level for concrete business cases have a more straightforward steering function. They are used to ensure that individual changes actually occur in the desired manner. They often have a narrower scope (e.g. a business unit, business domain or business program) and go into more depth in describing detail. They are designated by the expression *domain architecture* and may have a specific name, such as *retail architecture*.

Finally, the type of architecture that serves as a framework for a specific project is more directly concerned with the operational level. Once a positive business case has turned into a project, architecture is required to provide a framework within which design decisions are to be made. The emphasis is on the design: the guidelines and standards with which the project must comply, but also the delineation of projects and any questions concerning re-use that may arise. These architectures provide the degree of precise detail required by the project leader in order to have a sufficient basis on which to make appropriate design decisions for a particular project. This type of architecture is called *project-start architecture*.

Of course, these architectures do not exist separately from each other. In fact, they are different views of the same goal, providing different perspectives on the same circumstances for various purposes and target groups (Figure 4.8).

It is important to be aware of the differences in perspective. Being sensitive to the outlook of others increases the chance that the architecture being produced will be practical and well received by people other than those who have formulated it. Avoid the mistake of going into more depth than necessary, as well as the danger of providing excessive breadth in describing aspects that are irrelevant to the architecture's purpose.

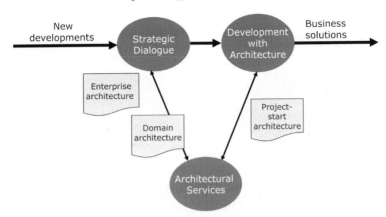

***Figure 4.8*** **Different architectural perspectives**

A university hospital has three important main functions: education, research and patient care. The employees of this hospital switch easily from one function to another. A doctor may be operating in the morning and lecturing in the afternoon.

The IT support system is, however, not geared to such flexibility. Each main function has its own systems and infrastructure. There is no structural provision for exchanging data. There is no collective vision of the IT support required to integrate these functions.

The hospital's annual plan recognizes the need for more collaboration between the functions. An enterprise architecture is drafted to make this collaboration happen. This EA contains descriptions of the most important processes in each main function and the data used in each. In this way, opportunities for collaboration readily emerge, such as the possibility of making anonymous patient data available to researchers. Infrastructural requirements are also identified, for which a collective policy can then be established.

The EA provides a framework to use in addressing the designated domains. First of all, the patient-care domain is to be addressed. A best-of-breed policy is chosen for this domain. Standard applications from various suppliers are used, and these applications have to communicate with each other. To implement and manage this policy for the patient-care domain, a domain architecture will be developed: the health-care architecture. This will be a service-based architecture stipulating the processes, data, and services that are needed as well as the applications that realize them.

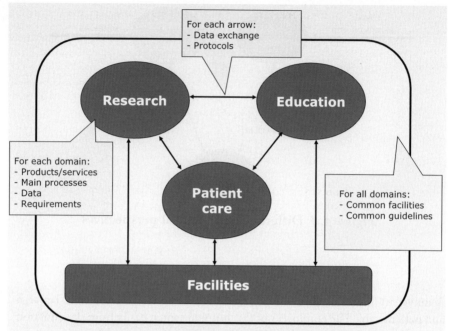

*Figure 4.9* **Hospital enterprise architecture**

Upon the initiation of a project to enable information exchange with GPs over the internet, the relevant principles and models are extracted from the enterprise and health-care architecture and assembled in a project-start architecture. They are then converted into design choices for the project.

Table 4.1 indicates a number of characteristic differences among the three perspectives of architecture. This table must be applied in a flexible manner. Not every architecture fits precisely into one of the columns. The purpose of the table is to alert people to the various perspectives to consider in formulating an architecture and the importance of carefully choosing among them. Moreover, there could be other target groups besides senior, middle and operational management, and a project-start architecture could be developed without architectural tools. Ultimately, the features can only be given substance in a specific situation.

## 4.6 Producing Effective Architecture

In developing architecture, the first step is to identify the changes that the organization has in store. This requires a good Strategic Dialogue, which is

*Table 4.1* **Comparison of the architectural perspectives**

| | *Strategic* | *Tactical* | *Operational* |
|---|---|---|---|
| *Purpose* | Support for decisions about "far-reaching" enterprise-wide business goals, priorities and infrastructural requirements | Support for decisions about the feasibility and achievability of a particular business goal | Provision of a concrete and goal-oriented framework for a project |
| *Target group* | Senior management | Middle management | Operational management |
| *Trigger* | Business goal with an extensive scope (e.g. new strategy) | Business goal with limited scope (e.g. introduction of a new product on the market) | Concrete project (e.g. implementation of a new product) |
| *Supports the production of* | Strategic documents, business cases or program proposals | Business cases, project proposals | (IT) solutions |
| *Language used* | "Dick & Jane" | "Bizz-talk" | "Tech-talk" |
| *Tools* | Powerpoint | Powerpoint & architectural tools | Architectural tools |
| *Focus* | Coherence and collaboration | Function (what) | Design (how) |
| *Scope* | Often organizationally determined: a branch, enterprise or division | Often determined by the business goal: the functional and technical areas that are affected by the business goal | Determined by the project: the delineation of the project |

the only way for the architects to develop a sufficient appreciation for the business goals, but also because it enables new opportunities to emerge from the architecture. In practice, Strategic Dialogue has various forms. It may be a planning and control cycle in which the business goals for the coming period are periodically established (e.g. in annual plans). In addition, new ideas will arise intermittently and this ad hoc idea generation should be supported by allowing Strategic Dialogue to occur at the appropriate time. The best way to bring this about is by building good relations with business.

The need served by architecture is based on current and expected business developments. This need can take many shapes. Senior management might want a "simple" scheme outlining the alignment of business programs. There may be a need to specify how new products are to be marketed or how a virtual work environment can be designed for all employees. Often an organization will work on several architectures at the same time, at any given time choosing to focus on one or more that most closely serve the needs of the organization at that time. This entails setting priorities to give precedence to those changes having the greatest impact on the organization. In practice, it may be that a project-start architecture is required for an important project without there being any existing domain or enterprise architecture. The determination of the architectural need is a continuous process.

Once the organization is clear about the needs that architectures should serve, the characteristics of each of the architectures can be determined. For example, the scope depends upon the degree of autonomy in the various business units. The aspects to be included depend upon the business goals. The introduction of a new product will require a detailed vision of processes, data and applications, while the technical architecture required may be quite evident. In establishing a virtual work environment to be used as a shared facility, the emphasis is primarily on middleware, platform and network. In the case of an organizational shake-up, not a single aspect may be left out and all the columns in the DYA framework must be given attention. Finally, the depth and form will be determined by considering the intended use and the proposed target group. For example, a high-level, abstract scheme for senior management is quite different from the concrete guidelines required by the software-development team.

The first step in developing an architecture is drafting an architecture Project Plan. It will ensure that sufficient attention is paid to all the dimensions described above before the architects turn to content. The Project Plan gives proper consideration to the purpose, nature and use of the architecture and provides a guideline during the architectural development to keep the project on target. In addition to the usual elements of such project plans, it will identify:

### 1 Sponsor

The sponsor for architecture is preferably someone from senior management. Searching for a sponsor outside the architecture team forces the architect to reflect on why the architecture is being developed and how to explain it clearly to the sponsor. This section also indicates the value of the architecture to be developed to the sponsor. It is essential that sponsors actively fulfill their roles and participate in discussing what precisely will be produced.

*2 Purpose and target group*
This section should briefly, concisely and as concretely as possible indicate what the organization will achieve by developing this architecture. The target group can be derived from the goal.

*3 Orientation*
An architecture has a certain orientation, which may describe a current situation (today architecture), plan for the future (tomorrow architecture), or be a combination of both. Furthermore, it makes a difference if a tomorrow architecture represents an ideal view of an unattainable goal or a concrete sketch of the way things must evolve – in nine months, for example. General principles and policy directives in an architecture can be regarded as compulsory regulations or simply guidelines. To prevent misunderstanding and confusion, it is important to be clear about the orientation of the proposed architecture.

*4 Use of the architecture*
The architecture being produced must suit the manner in which it is going to be used. Using it as a communications tool for senior management makes different demands than using it as a project framework does.

*5 Requirements of the architecture*
The requirements imposed on the planned architecture will be closely connected to its purpose and its target group. Requirements can, for example, involve the extent to which consideration must be given to developments outside the organization, the degree of detail that is desired or the aspects to be addressed.

*6 Scope of the architecture*
The scope of the proposed architecture may be the entire enterprise or merely a division or business unit.

*7 Content of the architecture*
The dimensions of aspect, form and depth are elaborated in this section. The aspects covered by the architecture are reported, and the precise deliverables are identified. The architecture could involve products/services, processes, organization, data, applications and/or technical infrastructure. The architecture might take the form of guidelines and/or models.

*8 The relation to other architectures*
How does the proposed architecture fit into the entire architectural scheme?

*9 Approach*
What approach is to be adopted in drafting the architecture? Which activities are to be performed and how much time devoted to them? Given the danger of architects becoming completely lost in models, time frames for drafting or delivering specific components of the architecture could be pre-set and monitored (time boxes).

*10 Stakeholders*
The stakeholders for the architecture are identified, as well as the manner in which they will be involved in the projected activities. If the stakeholders are closely involved in developing the architecture, that improves the knowledge base and also increases organizational support and buy-in for the architecture. For example, a focus group could be set up to review the content.

*11 Approval of the architecture*
Establishing in advance who must ultimately approve the architecture prevents the product from falling into limbo. It also discourages ongoing discussion about the architecture's validity and mandate. These discussions often prove to be a death blow for what, in itself, might be an extremely good plan.

*12 Maintenance of the architecture*
Designate individuals to maintain the proposed architecture once it is in place.

A Project Plan for the development of architecture will ensure that the above items are given timely consideration. Many architects concentrate on content, which is fine so long as the content serves a clear purpose and garners both support and acceptance. However, there is an enormous risk that the architect may become immersed in content, overshoot the goal and deliver a product for which there is no support. For that reason it is extremely important to draft a Project Plan in advance.

　　When the architect delivers the product it should be appreciatively received and also actively employed. At the start of the architecture trajectory and also at its conclusion is it important to pay attention to how the results will be incorporated into the organization. This can be done by accompanying the delivery with practical advice. If, for example, the purpose of the architecture is to investigate the possibilities of synergy, the architect can, at this point, make recommendations about the areas in which synergy is possible.

## 4.7  An Architectural Framework Encompasses All Architectures

Architecture is developed on the basis of business goals. In general, an organization does not have one architecture but a collection of them. This set of architectures must be managed. An architectural framework, like the DYA framework, provides a means of doing this. It is an especially practical way of structuring architectures. Such a framework can be regarded as a series of pigeonholes in which all the architectural artifacts can be organized.

The dimensions of aspect and form are represented in the framework by the columns and rows. The dimension of scope can be visualized as a hierarchy of frameworks, as shown in Figure 4.10.

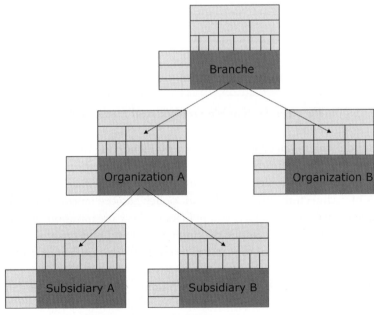

*Figure 4.10* **Hierarchy of frameworks**

The DYA framework has proven in practice to be an efficient mechanism for managing various architectures. Some organizations may already have their own

*Building an Enterprise Architecture Practice*

specific sets of terminology, and should adapt this framework to their familiar terms. In particular, we find that the columns in the framework (the aspect areas) may vary from organization to organization.

Architectural practices are introduced into one of the subsidiaries of a multinational organization. In particular, the DYA architectural framework is introduced as the basis for architectural development and management. It turns out that the parent company already employs a standard classification of technological domains. This classification is applied to the framework. It is also evident that the need for IT support in this organization is fully determined by the business processes and their use of data. This resulted in the following framework:

| | Business objectives | | | | | | | | |
|---|---|---|---|---|---|---|---|---|---|
| | Information Architecture | | IT Architecture | | | | | | |
| | Process | Data | Appli-cation | Plat-form | Desk-top | Data-base | Middle-ware | Develop-ment | System Mana-gement |
| Principles | | | | | | | | | |
| Policy directives | | | | | | | | | |
| Models | | | | | | | | | |

***Figure 4.11* Sample architectural framework**

One of the issues in managing architecture is identifying the set of architectures that an organization already possesses. In every organization, even those not officially employing architecture, there are artifacts present that may perform the function of architecture: strategic choices, policy choices, norms and standards. Additionally, there are principles and policies in every organization that may not be stated explicitly but are implicitly employed when projects are initiated. An architecture framework helps to map and to position these explicit and sometimes implicit architectures.

In an organization beginning to work with architecture, it is advisable to involve the designated architects in positioning the architectural documents already existing within the overall framework. This helps the architect to conceptualize the architecture and its role. Moreover, it might reveal that implicit architecture is already in use. If so, the explicit application of architecture may not seem like such a large step, and the initial release of the architecture can be quickened.

One of the first steps to be taken by an organization wishing to professionalize its architectural practices is to take an inventory of what already exists in the way of architectural artifacts. This is best done in a workshop attended by the organization's architects to be. In this example, the inventory produces the following result:

*Table 4.2* **Sample architectural artifacts**

| No. | Architecture |
|-----|--------------|
| 1 | Master plan in development |
| 11 | Master plan until 2004 |
| 14 | I&A plan 1998–2002 |
| 15 | Information planning for divisions |
| 2 | Network landscape (as is) |
| 3 | Integration server (*de facto* standard) |
| 4 | N-tier model |
| 5 | Architectural Review |
| 6 | Conditions for connecting to the network |
| 16 | Security guidelines (external communication) |
| 7 | Application landscape (as is) |
| 8 | Organization chart |
| 9 | Implicit criteria from the technical architects |
| 10 | Guidelines for specific projects |
| 12 | Guidelines & frameworks in various advisory reports |
| 13 | Requirements of the IT program |

Subsequently, the architects positioned these architectural artifacts in a DYA architectural framework in which the numbers refer to the above-mentioned architectural products.

*Building an Enterprise Architecture Practice*

*Table 4.3* **Sample mapping of architectural artifacts in an architectural framework**

| | Business objectives | | | | | | | |
|---|---|---|---|---|---|---|---|---|
| | Business architecture | | | Information architecture | | Technical architecture | | |
| | Prod. / Service | Process | Organi-zation | Data | Application | Middleware | Platform | Network |
| General principles | 1, 5, 10, 12, 13, 14 | | | | | | | |
| Policy directives | 5, 10, 12 | | | 4, 5, 10, 12 | | 4, 5, 6, 9 | | |
| Models | 8, 15 | | | 7, 11, 15 | | 2, 3 | | |

The discussion resulting from the inventory and positioning ultimately led to the following conclusions:

— there is a relatively large amount of policy but only a few models;

— the architecture is fragmented; it is, for the most part, buried in plans, reports and recommendations;

— there is a lot of implicit criteria;

— there is relatively little in the way of *business architecture* (processes and organization).

In organizations that have been employing architecture for some time, the framework can help bring order to the architectural totality. This may, for example, come into play after a merger, when the merging companies bring their own architectures with them. The framework is useful in mapping out the architectural terrain, detecting overlaps and identifying what needs to be continued and what must be modified. It provides a means of combining the best from both corporate worlds.

## 4.8 An Enterprise Architecture for B-Sure Bank

Anne's questions to Kevin about his key diagram of B-Sure Bank's future organization caused Arnold Hedges, the head of the architecture task force, to do some serious thinking. This scheme was good – he was sure of that. It was also very useful in identifying the possibilities for synergy. But it had been developed in relative isolation by two of his architects. The reasons for various choices and the precise consequences of the scheme were not clear to everyone. Furthermore, the scheme did not have any formal status. It certainly functioned as a sort of "framework" for the task force, but it would be nice if all of B-Sure Bank adopted it. Perhaps they ought to work on that a bit.

OK, Arnold decided, we need a well-supported architecture somewhat resembling a "city plan." Seems like a good job for Mary. Let's get her to draft a Project Plan. And Fred could certainly help out.

Two weeks later, the draft Project Plan lay on Arnold's desk.

---

**Project Plan for B-Sure Bank Enterprise Architecture (EA)**

*1 Sponsor*
The sponsor is the board of directors. It will use the architecture to achieve its synergy objectives.

*2 Purpose and target group*
The EA has the purpose of clarifying where opportunities for synergy lie, insofar as both processes and applications are concerned, and how these opportunities are to be exploited.

The EA will primarily serve as a communications tool for management. The target groups for the EA are therefore primarily the board of directors and management. Additionally, the EA will be used to communicate the vision of information supply to the rest of B-Sure Bank. For the architects, the EA is the reference framework for all other architectures.

*3 Orientation*
The EA does not sketch the as-is state but the to-be scenario that B-Sure Bank wants to realize. The rate at which that should occur has not, at present, been determined. For the time being, the horizon of the development scheme is set at five years. The board of directors expects the architecture task force to indicate, on the basis of this plan, which changes need to occur in what order of priority.

*4 Use of the architecture*
The EA will be primarily used to allocate the responsibilities for processes and applications to the appropriate areas of the new organization. In this sense, it is

---

a communications tool for the new management and will be used by the board of directors to communicate their plans.

### 5  Requirements of the architecture

The following requirements are being imposed on the architecture:

— the EA must be in step with the organizational shake-up that is currently taking place

— it must support the objectives concerning increased sales and expanded customer base

— there must be a good balance between central control and decentralized autonomy – the primary guideline in this regard is the principle of having responsibility and authority as low in the organization as possible

At least the following questions must be answered by the EA:

— Which products/services can be combined and to what advantage?

— Which business functions can be combined and to what advantage?

— Which business processes can be combined and to what advantage?

— Which applications can be dismantled and to what advantage?

— What is the best way of dealing with customer data?

— Which infrastructural facilities must be provided to all divisions of B-Sure Bank?

### 6  Scope of the architecture

The scope of the EA is the entire B-Sure Bank, though limited to the internal B-Sure Bank organization. Interfaces with other institutions, such as the Federal Reserve are outside the EA's scope.

### 7  Content of the architecture

The EA will consist of the following components.

(i)  *Subdivision of B-Sure Bank into business domains* (the existing general diagram will be taken as the starting point):

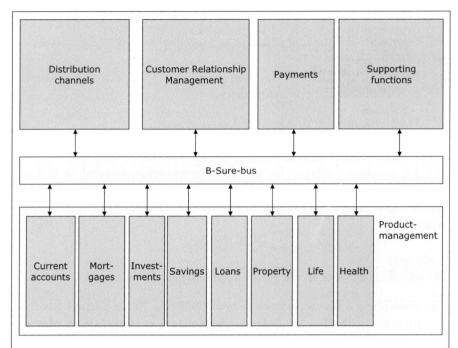

*Figure 4.12* **Subdivision into domains at B-Sure Bank**

This diagram has to be verified.

(ii) *For each business domain*:

   – products/services that the domain provides;

   – demands that the domain makes on its processes and information supply;

   – general description of the domain in terms of processes, data and applications.

(iii) *Interdependence of domains*:

   – data exchange;

   – protocols.

(iv)  *Centralized-decentralized balance*:

  – shared facilities;
  – shared regulations and guidelines.

(v)  *Mapping of the as-is state onto the business domains*

### 8  The relation to other architectures

The EA provides guidance for all the changes being initiated at B-Sure Bank. This means that other architectures must comply with and fit into this framework. All other architectures can be seen as elaborations of various parts of the EA.

### 9  Approach

The following activities will be performed in implementing the EA:

(i)  *Establishing a Communication Matrix (16 hours)*: Since it is not possible to draft architecture in isolation, formulate a communication plan to ensure that the right parties receive the right information at the right time. Interviews with key decision makers and specialists will have a place in the communication plan.

(ii)  *Analysis of as-is state (32 hours)*: Map the current distribution channels, customer groups, product groups and support functions over the existing divisions. This produces the following table (to be completed and verified):

**Table 4.4  Analysis of the overlaps involving B-Sure Bank divisions**

|                              | B-Bank | Virtuality | Personality |
|------------------------------|:------:|:----------:|:-----------:|
| Distribution: local branch   |   X    |            |      X      |
| Distribution: internet       |        |     X      |             |
| Distribution: call center    |        |     X      |      X      |
| Distribution: mail           |        |     X      |      X      |
| Distribution: agents         |   X    |            |      X      |
| Distribution: ATM            |        |     X      |      X      |

| | B-Bank | Virtuality | Personality |
|---|---|---|---|
| Customer management: private individuals | | X | X |
| Customer management: businesses | X | | X |
| Product: current accounts | X | X | X |
| Product: mortgages | | X | X |
| Product: investments | X | X | X |
| Product: savings | | X | X |
| Product: loans | X | X | X |
| Product: property and casualty insurance | | | X |
| Product: life insurance | | | X |
| Product: health insurance | | | X |
| Support: payment transactions | X | X | X |
| Support: other support functions | X | X | X |

(iii) *Verification of basic diagram (48 hours)*: Verify the proposed domains by interviewing department heads and process owners.

(iv) *Elaboration of basic diagram (240 hours)*: Further elaborate the domains in terms of the items mentioned in Section 7 of this Project Plan. For this purpose, there will be a great deal of discussion with relevant experts in the organization.

(v) *Feedback on the architecture (32 hours)*: Review the details of the EA in a number of workshops involving the individuals previously interviewed and other relevant experts.

(vi) *Mapping of the as-is state (80 hours)*: Map the current processes, applications and organizational components onto the architectural domains.

(vii) *EA approval (12 hours)*: Submit the architecture for approval by the board of directors. This will be accompanied by a presentation.

The projected time schedule is 15 weeks.

*10 Stakeholders*
The following parties will be involved in developing the EA:

- departmental managers of existing divisions;

- process owners;

- information managers;

- IT managers.

### 11 *Final approval of the architecture*
The EA will be submitted to the board of directors for final approval.

### 12 *Maintenance of the architecture*
The architecture task force will manage and maintain the EA.

### 13 *Project organization*
The project team consists of Mary Bates, Kevin McAndrew and Fred Brooks. Progress will be monitored by a steering group consisting of:

- Arnold Hedges, head of the architecture task force;

- Peter Wilder, Director of Personality;

- Peter Bennett, Manager of Personality Property and Casualty;

- Irene Cooper, Manager of Virtuality Investments;

- William Hawthorne, process owner of product development at B-Bank.

# 5 A SWOT ANALYSIS OF THE PROCESS

In its ultimate form, architecture gives an organization the power to respond quickly and effectively to change. The capacity to respond effectively requires a combination of thought and action. Two instruments, the Quadrant Model and the DYA Model, can analyze an organization's capabilities in this regard.

## 5.1 Things Are Not All Right at B-Sure Bank

"I believe wholeheartedly in the importance of architecture," said Peter Wilder, one of the directors at B-Sure Bank, "But I see too little bang for my buck. The vision document that you drafted is clear. I back it entirely. Still, you've been working on it for nearly a year. You've assembled a good team of 15 architects. The service architecture that your people have created is good. Yet, although the diagrams are posted on all the walls, I don't see any further effects. I recently spoke with a project manager who knew the diagram well but didn't know what he was supposed to do with it. When I discussed this with another project manager, I heard the same story. I am starting to have misgivings. Or is that just me?"

Arnold Hedges, now the head of the new Architecture department, did not know how to respond. He certainly understood the feeling of unease that his boss was having. His team was working extremely hard, but things were getting bogged down somewhere. Everyone appeared to be positive about the architecture concept, and people were even eager to talk about it. So why did he have the feeling that the pay-off was not as big as it should be? Was enough attention being paid to the project managers? Or was it just a question of time?

"Give me another six months," he appealed to Peter. "We just require more time. It's an adjustment for the organization as well. We still have to learn how to adopt architectural thinking in a truly effective manner."

## 5.2  Architectural Practice: A Question of Thought and Action

Developing architectures that are appropriate and in sync with business goals is not enough. For the organization to put architecture into effective practice, it must on the one hand be integrated into a business strategy. On the other hand, architectural thinking must be incorporated into projects and operations. If equal amounts of consideration are given to both requirements, good things will happen, but any feeling that architectural practice does not do what it is supposed to likely indicates an imbalance between theory and practice.

A SWOT analysis of architectural practice provides some insight into this situation and lays the foundation for improvement. As a result, the organization gains a better hold on the situation, something more than the mere hope of improvement in six months.

Two instruments can be used to sketch a clear picture of how the architectural processes in an organization are actually doing. Both analyses can be done in a short time.

— The Quadrant Model is employed, especially at the management level, in order to quickly represent the state of an organization's architectural practices.

— The DYA Model allows the stakeholders in the architecture to consider the extent to which the architectural processes have been effectively implemented.

## 5.3  The Quadrant Model: A Quick Scan of Thought and Action

The Quadrant Model, introduced in Wagter *et al.* [25] and reproduced in Figure 5.1, has proven to be a tool that swiftly indicates the extent to which the architecture is aligned with the business strategy and the degree to which it is incorporated into projects and operations. The positioning of the organization in the Quadrant Model provides an initial assessment of the situation and offers a basis for further progress. It is primarily a communications tool meant to demonstrate why certain practices occur in the way that they do, and it points to improvements that can be made.

The Quadrant Model simultaneously measures the relationship between two dimensions:

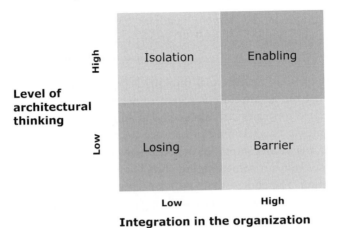

***Figure 5.1* Quadrant Model**

— The level of architectural thinking indicates the degree to which the upper strata of the organization's business and IT domains share an architectural vision and appreciate the importance of architectural practices.

— The degree of integration within the organization reveals the extent to which architectural thinking is embodied in the organization's daily processes. Architecture lives to the extent that there is an awareness of it on the work floor and it is incorporated into daily practices.

Plotting these dimensions along vertical and horizontal axes produces four quadrants:

1. Organizations in the *losing* quadrant have a low level of architectural thinking and a low degree of organizational integration. Architectural practices do not have any real effect on this organization.

2. Organizations in the *barrier* quadrant have taken architectural measures but in a fragmented manner and not on the basis of a shared organization-wide vision.

3. Organizations in the *isolation* quadrant are fully convinced, right up to the most senior levels, of the importance of architecture. The architecture is clearly related to business goals. Architectural practices are, however, insufficiently embedded within the organization's processes of change.

4. Organizations in the *enabling* quadrant have integrated their architecture and demonstrate a high level of architectural thinking. In this quadrant, organizations are free to work on continued improvement and renewal.

When the level of architectural thinking is high, the organization has a clear vision of what the architecture is meant to accomplish. Architectural thinking is closely related to strategic thinking, and architectural content is geared to the business strategy. The relationship between architectures and business goals is clear. There is a clear process for architectural development and management. Architecture is not just something for the IT department, but involves business and IT together. The entire issue is well conceptualized.

When organizational integration is high, the organization "works under architecture." The architecture is not a paper tiger but a factor with significance for projects and operations. Managers and employees are aware of the architecture, use it when making decisions and adopt its frameworks. Architectural practice is a part of the organizational culture. It is as natural as project planning and system documentation.

Table 5.1 contains an Architectural Review, a simple test to determine the quadrant in which an organization is located. The first six statements in the table measure the level of architectural thinking. Is architectural development truly driven by business goals? Is the architecture up to date? And is sufficient attention paid to the architectural development process? The last six statements measure the degree of organizational integration. Is the architecture accessible? Do projects comply with the architecture? Does architecture play a role in decision making?

The number of times statements 1 through 6 are answered "yes" indicates the vertical position in the model. The number of "yes" answers to statements 7 through 12 reveals the horizontal position.

## 5.4  Isolation: Too Much Thought, Too Little Action

Organizations in the isolation quadrant have a good conception of architecture. They have a clear vision of its importance and purpose. Architectural choices are directly related to the business strategy and goals. The architects are strongly focused on the business managers and strategists in the organization; they are on easy terms with each other. The architects stand on equal footing with business. Briefly stated, everything runs smoothly insofar as content is concerned. However, the architecture is not incorporated into projects and operations. The architects do not bother to ensure that the architectural principles are adopted in concrete

### *Table 5.1* **Architectural Review**

| No. | Statement | Yes/No |
|---|---|---|
| 1 | In our organization, architecture is a part of the management agenda | Yes/No |
| 2 | A new version of our organization's architecture has been issued in recent years | Yes/No |
| 3 | Architects and business representatives are in regular contact with each other | Yes/No |
| 4 | I think that at least half of the architectural initiatives in our organization have a business sponsor | Yes/No |
| 5 | I know which director is responsible for architecture | Yes/No |
| 6 | Our architectural process is regularly evaluated | Yes/No |
| 7 | I think that at least a quarter of the organization has immediate access to the most recent version of the architecture | Yes/No |
| 8 | In our organization, architecture plays an important role in decisions about projects | Yes/No |
| 9 | An architect is involved in at least half of the projects at our organization | Yes/No |
| 10 | Our architects have a customer-focused attitude | Yes/No |
| 11 | Completion of a project is only acknowledged after an architectural review has been performed on the project | Yes/No |
| 12 | Non-compliance with architecture results at least in being asked to justify the non-compliance | Yes/No |

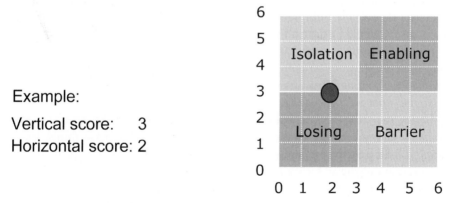

*Figure 5.2* **Positioning an organization in the Quadrant Model**

projects. They simply assume that the projects will comply with the architecture. The nitty-gritty details are typically left up to the project teams.

The great danger here is that project teams must use a disproportionate amount of effort to satisfy the architectural requirements. In most cases like this, so much effort is demanded that the sponsor and project manager privately agree to recognize architecture's failings and to rely on other resources in finding a workable solution.

These are the organizations where architects appear to sit in those well-known ivory towers. The organizations know what they want but fail to achieve it.

The information manager at a lease company has come to the conclusion that an architecture is needed to manage all the changes that are about to happen. He invites an architect to come and discuss how best to achieve this. During the interview, the architect asks if this is the first attempt at architecture. The information manager answers that something was indeed done by his predecessor but that was a couple of years ago now. At that time, a specialist was brought in for the task, and an architectural model was made. The diagrams are still hanging in the hall. And there has to be a document somewhere. But honestly speaking, he is not abiding by it in any way, and the same goes for his employees. In any case, he cannot find anyone who knows its specifics. To him, it seemed better to start all over again.

In concluding that it is better to make a new beginning, the information manager is probably right. Since the developers of the architecture had left the company, it would be difficult to inject any new life into the existing documents – not to mention that they are most certainly out of date. The entire process will therefore have to be gone through again with the current employees and with an eye to today's business strategy.

If the information manager wants to prevent the new architecture from suffering the same fate, he will have to approach things in a different manner. With so many changes of the guard, it is no longer clear how things were done in the past, but it looks like a great deal of attention was paid to the composition of the architecture's content without considering how it would be incorporated into the organization. The architecture was never converted into action. This time, the information manager must endeavor not only to develop architecture but also to devote at least as much time and effort to the integration of architectural thinking throughout the organization.

## 5.5 Barrier: Restricted to Efficiency

The barrier quadrant involves the opposite. The architecture is a living component in projects, but there is no connection to the strategic vision. The architecture stems from a sense of method and professionalism among the designers and developers. It is primarily aimed at streamlining projects as well as integrating applications and technology. Standardization is an important element but is often limited to a single department. Because the architecture is, in a sense, created from the bottom up, a situation might arise where several competing architectures are not in alignment with each other. And since no control is being exercised from a top-down business viewpoint, it is difficult to justify the architectural choices that have been made. As a consequence, discussions about the correct architectural principles can be lengthy and difficult to resolve. An organization can find itself positioned in the barrier quadrant as a result of a merger in which each party throws its own architecture into the pot. In such a case, the development of a collective top-down vision will be the only way to unify these architectures.

Organizations in the barrier quadrant run the risk of becoming fixated on continuously improving efficiency without improving effectiveness. Things are done well but it remains unclear whether the right things are being done.

The directors of a retail organization have decided that the organization needs an architecture to coordinate its operations. A consultant is engaged to oversee it. In interviews with employees, the consultant notes their slightly surprised reactions. The employees do not understand the decision. Haven't they had architecture for a while? However, further questioning reveals that each employee has a different notion of what architecture is. For one person, it is a data model set up a few years ago for the core system. For another, it is a number of design principles that were established in a department sometime in the past. A third individual believes that an architecture might exist but it is not suited to the organization's new IT developments, so this employee is busy drafting principles to guide the new developments.

The above scenario is typical of the barrier quadrant. Architectural principles are established in all sorts of places based on individual skills and applied to the immediate environment. However, there is no coherence among the various models, rules and guidelines.

A good first step in such a case would be to map the various architectures that already exist – by positioning them in the DYA architecture framework, for example. A second step would then establish the connection to the business strategy. Inconsistencies and principles that are no longer supportive of the business goals would subsequently be eliminated. In this way, principles that are demonstrably up to date would receive stronger support. If the organization wishes to employ architecture to its fullest potential, it should expend energy in initiating dialogue between business and IT. Such a dialogue would develop a central vision as a basis for steering architectural developments.

## 5.6  Losing: The Case for Architecture

In the losing quadrant, architecture is not being given any consideration at all. Some individuals may be aware of the importance of architecture, but this view is not shared by the entire organization. Organizations placed in this quadrant have to ask themselves if their lack of concern with architecture is appropriate. So long as they exist in a stable environment, it is possible to do without architecture. The relevance of architecture only becomes evident when fundamental changes are occurring or when the business operation is, perhaps gradually, becoming increasingly more complex. The problem is that by the time such changes become apparent, the need for architecture is often extremely acute. To avoid that crisis, organizations in this quadrant should reflect a little and ask themselves if it might not be wise to introduce architectural thinking.

Organizations in the losing quadrant face the key question what they wish to accomplish by employing architecture.

An employee of a utility company has noticed that a proliferation of applications has been created over the years. All these applications are linked to each other in a most divergent manner, and data is continuously shuffled from right to left and back again. This situation is a nearly inevitable consequence of the relaxed culture dominant in the organization. When the business requires support from an information system, an application manager or an IT employee is asked to provide it. And they are happy to comply. No mechanism for coordination or alignment has been put in place. Up to this point, everything has worked out fine. But with the extensive changes that are expected in the next little while, the employee sees a large continuity risk in this practice. He is convinced that there has to be more coherence and structure in information management.

The employee in this example sees the dangers arising from the continuation of the old practices: the information flows threaten to become so complex that instituting the pending changes will be extremely difficult. He views architectural thinking as a means of reducing complexity and, therefore, increasing flexibility.

However, this will require a substantial cultural turnaround. The employee chooses a gradual route: he begins by closely examining data management. In this way, he is soon able to identify a number of significant improvements. While mobilizing his fellow workers to effect these improvements, he simultaneously works on enhancing awareness within the organization. His goal is to broaden the architecture one step at a time.

## 5.7 Enabling: Room for Quality

The level of architectural awareness and the degree of architectural integration are both high in the enabling quadrant. The organization knows what it wants in the way of architecture and accomplishes it. There is a clear purpose and vision concerning architectural practice. The architectural initiatives are directly linked to strategic issues and choices. It is natural for projects to comply with architecture, not just because the life of the project manager is easier as a result, but because such compliance assures the sponsor that the right solution to his or her problem is chosen. Briefly stated, the architecture works and does what it is supposed to do.

In a telecommunications company, the employment of architecture has become standard practice. All business projects start with the drafting of a project-start architecture. A team of eight business and IT architects develop the architecture according to set plans and with fixed time frames. In this way, sponsors always know precisely where they are in terms of planning. At any moment, the team of architects is working on three project-start architectures. Every four weeks, a new project-start architecture can be initiated. In formulating project-start architectures, the architects work from a collective architecture framework. In particular, this framework is concerned with integration aspects, as the company works almost exclusively with software application packages. Due to the efficient work procedures and predictable time frames, the department has gained a great deal of credibility with business managers and is progressively more involved in concept development.

Right from the start, this architecture department has focused on embedding the architecture within the organization. The architects are involved in development projects and, from this position, work on bringing architectural thinking to a higher level. This was a good choice given the critical importance in the telecommunications sector of reacting quickly to market developments. Gradually, a clear and shared vision of architecture has been created and aligned with the business strategy, as the company little by little enters the enabling quadrant.

## 5.8  *Learning from the Position in the Quadrant Model*

In large organizations, it is not unusual to encounter characteristics from more than one quadrant. A frequent combination involves both isolation and barrier. For example, this combination will occur in organizations that not only have a central architecture department operating as a discrete unit but also have the business units performing one or more architecture functions. In such cases, the central architecture department is primarily concerned with the translation of the overall business strategy into rather abstract architectural models and principles for the entire organization. Here, the greatest danger is isolation. The architects working in the various business units are much more preoccupied with making architectural choices to serve concrete business projects. They work primarily from the bottom up, running the risk of entering the barrier quadrant, each unit having its own architecture. If there is no link between the centralized architecture and the architectures of the individual business units, this can result in a great deal of mutual misunderstanding and acting at cross-purposes. This is unfortunate because, if the two perspectives were combined instead of working in opposition to each other, the organization would move a lot closer to the enabling quadrant.

The following example demonstrates that the Quadrant Model can help subsidiaries learn from each other.

Two subsidiaries of the same international holding company have both been using architecture for years. One followed a top-down approach in its architectural practices and established a central architecture department. Based on a vision for the business, architects successively developed a domain architecture, process architecture, data architecture and application architecture. These architectures have been well integrated but, in practice, project results regularly turn out to be poorly compatible. In part, this appears to result from the fact that a lot of reinterpretation is required in order to make concrete project decisions based upon the architecture.

The second subsidiary employed an entirely different, bottom-up approach. Because it became apparent that the business was not successfully engaging in strategic discussions, it was decided to standardize the technical infrastructure. Together with the specialists in this area, the architects formulated principles and policies. Since the system developers are actively collaborating in the development of architecture, its translation into projects occurs almost effortlessly. Policy and implementation are in the same hands. Streamlining the technical infrastructure is entirely successful, but the subsidiary does not succeed in taking the next step to greater effectiveness. This would require the participation of the business domain.

Positioning both subsidiaries in the Quadrant Model indicates that the first one is in the isolation and the second in the barrier quadrant. Once they perceive each other's positioning, they immediately realize that they have a lot to offer each other and could learn a great deal from a mutual exchange of experiences. Both are enjoying partial success, but neither can make any further progress. Since the one has what the other is lacking, they have a terrific opportunity to exchange best practices and to learn from each other.

Plotting positions in the Quadrant Model proves to be, in practice, an extremely effective means of recording the status of architecture in the organization. In particular, it provides insight into the thought and action involved in architectural practices. It holds a mirror up to the organization.

## 5.9 The DYA Model: Further Analysis of Thought and Action

The Quadrant Model can be used to reveal the balance between visionary content and practical application. It indicates the sectors in which an organization's strengths and weaknesses lie in terms of its architectural practices. If the organization senses that architecture is not delivering on its promises, then plotting the architecture in its quadrant clearly demonstrates where things are out of whack.

The DYA Model (Figure 5.3) can be used to further analyze the position plotted in the Quadrant Model. The DYA Model analyzes the processes involved in architectural practices. For those individuals directly involved in implementing the architecture, this analysis provides insight into their roles as well as feedback on the strengths and weaknesses of their performances.

An analysis using the DYA Model reveals the circumstances behind the positioning in the Quadrant Model. An organization placed in the isolation quadrant will have the relationship between Architectural Services and Strategic Dialogue well in hand. The architecture is well aligned with the business strategy.

The relationship between Architectural Services and Development with(out) Architecture is, however, too insubstantial. The resulting risk is that projects must continually establish their own individual link to the business strategy, a process resulting in a great deal of inefficiency.

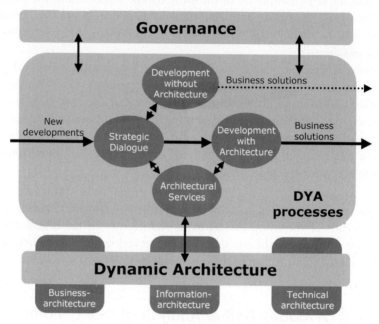

*Figure 5.3* **DYA Model**

For an organization in the barrier quadrant, the situation is reversed. In such a case, the architecture function is generally well suited to Development with(out) Architecture, but architecture plays hardly any role in the Strategic Dialogue. The resulting danger is that the wrong investments may be made.

In the losing quadrant, all the DYA processes require improvement. In the enabling quadrant, everything is in place, although fine tuning may still be necessary.

Regardless of the quadrant in which an organization is placed, it is always advisable to subject processes to careful examination. This can best be done by the people directly involved. The DYA Model provides a frame of reference with which to conduct such an analysis. An analysis based on this model yields insight into the manner in which architectural practices are given substance in the organization, each individual's personal role in these practices and the blanks that need to be filled in.

A good way to undertake this analysis involves a workshop for all those involved with architecture: business and IT management, project managers, architects and developers. This quickly yields positive results and has the additional advantage of bringing people together in order to discuss existing work procedures. Consequently, basic assumptions are often viewed in a new light.

The approach is as follows: the participants are divided into groups and are given a part of the DYA Model printed on a large sheet of paper (see Figure 5.4 for an example); each part represents one of the processes (Strategic Dialogue, Architectural Services or Development with(out) Architecture).

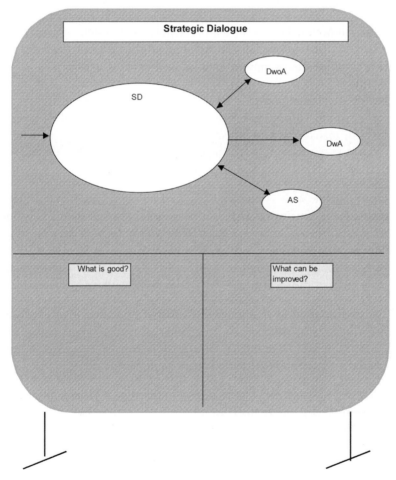

*Figure 5.4* **Part of the DYA Model for the sake of analysis**

The groups are then required to visualize the relevant process, such as it is currently being performed in the organization, and to describe it, including its interfaces with other processes. Using cardboard cards in various shapes and colors, felt pens and stickers, the situation can be effectively represented and visualized in an easily understandable manner. Moreover, the use of such materials stimulates thought. The groups work with the following concrete questions:

— How is the process currently being done?

— What is well done?

— What could be better?

Aspects that need to be examined are stakeholders, products, activities, triggers and governance. The groups subsequently present the different processes to each other. The resulting discussion can produce further refinements.

In a health-care institution that wants to make its use of architecture more effective, powerful and professional, one of the first steps involves holding a workshop for management, architects and developers in order to examine how the DYA processes are being performed. Analyzing the process of Development with(out) Architecture yields the following results:

— Development with Architecture is performed by the central strategy department. This works well, not because the organization has included architecture in a standard approach to development, because it has not, but only because they informally share working methods. In brief, its success here is strongly dependent on people. The decentralized development in other parts of the institution largely takes place without architecture.

— The Architectural Services process is not explicitly present in the institution. According to the participants, this process is actually more or less incorporated into the Development-with-Architecture process. Architecture is created in the context of, and as a part of, projects.

— It is unclear what the governing rules are: who, for example, actually determines what the architecture is?

The participants draw the diagram presented in Figure 5.5.

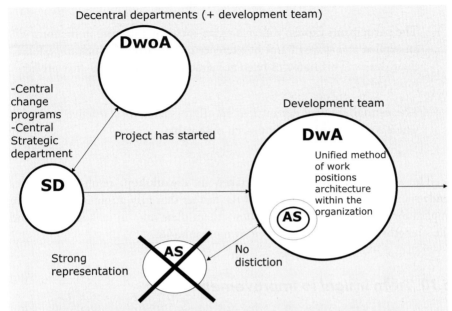

***Figure 5.5*  Analysis of development with(out) architecture**

What is well done?

— There is clear input from Strategic Dialogue.

— Participants are architecturally aware (especially the central strategy department).

What could be better?

— Develop architecture before a project starts (instead of during the project).

— Make architecture more explicit.

— Set up a form of governance.

In closing the workshop, the following conclusions are drawn:

— For employees of the central strategy department, architecture is primarily an implicit concern. They operate according to informal frameworks and an implicit sense of quality. There is no explicit architecture function and no collective framework.

— The participants express a clear longing for an architecture in the form of an explicit and shared frame of reference on the basis of which to perform their duties. This frame of reference should contain criteria that projects must satisfy.

— The central strategy department mostly operates in a reactive manner, whereas a more proactive approach is desirable.

The analysis of processes, undertaken in a workshop, results in a better understanding among stakeholders of the factors that play a role in the effective application of architecture. It also shows them their roles in its application and the strengths and weaknesses in their own organization.

## 5.10  From Insight to Improvement

The Quadrant Model and the DYA Model are tools to provide insight into an organization's strengths and weaknesses insofar as its employment of architecture is concerned. In particular, they clarify the balance between the architecture's alignment with business strategy and its relevance to projects. They promote understanding and can show where improvements are most needed.

For organizations wishing to make their architectural practices more effective and professional, we will provide an instrument in the next chapter to devise improvements suited to the circumstances of any particular organization. In essence this instrument, the Architecture Maturity Matrix, not only identifies the improvements to be made but also supports them by setting priorities in such a way that both thought and action receive proper attention. All this is done while keeping in mind that not everything can be done at once, nor needs to be.

## 5.11  SWOT Analysis at B-Sure Bank

It is one year since the merger, and B-Sure Bank is "still going strong." The shake-up has reached its conclusion, at least organizationally. All departments having similar roles have been combined into shared service centers. These are divided into Banking, Insurance and Investment. Due to the importance that the bank attaches to its customer relations, a separate Relations Management division has been created, which distinguishes between business and consumer clients on account of the difference in approach. All IT services have been removed from the various divisions and concentrated in the IT division. Figure 5.6 represents the new organizational chart.

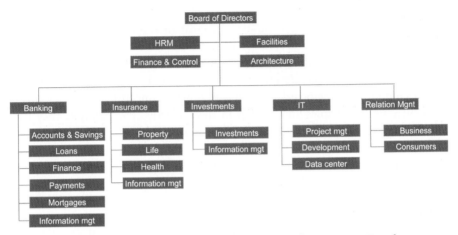

*Figure 5.6* **New organizational chart for B-Sure Bank**

In terms of processes and information systems, there is still a long way to go. But things are on the right track. In the technical arena, a communication bus has been established. It is the intention that all interaction between applications will occur by means of this bus. The first application will soon be connected to it.

Fifteen architects work as a team in the Architecture department. They are subdivided into business/information architects (7) and technical architects (8). They are responsible for the architecture of the B-Sure Bank.

Until now, the architects have produced a number of architectural distributables, which have been placed on the intranet:

— an overall B-Sure Bank enterprise architecture;

— a B-Sure Bank process model;

— a services model indicating the generic application services;

— guidelines for data modeling;

— guidelines for platform choices;

— guidelines for package selection and implementation;

—  an application architecture for Insurance;

—  a business architecture for Banking.

All the architecture documents are now formally approved prior to publication. Approvals are performed by an *architecture board* consisting of the IT director and the directors of Banking, Insurance, Investment and Relations Management. The board is chaired by the director of Insurance and bears the responsibility for the developments in the architectural field at B-Sure Bank. The architecture board meets twice a year. Besides approving any architectural documents that have been produced, the board can issue assignments concerning the development of architectural principles and models in specific areas. For example, they have recently assigned the task of developing data architecture.

In addition to being given assignments by the architecture board, the architects also develop architectural artifacts on their own initiative. They do this in response to business developments but also as a result of developments in the field of IT. The 15 architects are spread over four divisions, with a team of around four architects maintaining contact with each division. Each team handles this contact in its own manner. For example, every month the team for Banking has an informal lunch with the division's Information Manager. At these lunches, they discuss new developments. In Investment, contact occurs on a more personal basis: each architect has his or her own contacts in Investment and, whenever there is something to report or ask, they call each other up. Someone from the team for Relations Management knows the director of Relations Management well, and contact is primarily maintained through this channel. And in Insurance, contact mainly occurs between a member of the architecture team and the head of the Information Management department.

The idea is for projects to comply with the architectures. When a new architecture document is produced, it is brought to the attention of project managers by means of a newsletter. In practice, not all projects adhere to the architecture.

To make it easier for projects to comply with the architecture, architects together with a delegation of project managers and information analysts have carefully examined the quality of architectural products during a two-day retreat. Improvements have been made. An agreement has been reached to organize a similar gathering every year, as it has become evident that some changes tend to be overlooked in the course of daily events. For instance, outdated components are not being cleared out.

The architecture team is subdivided into two groups: the business/information architects and the technical architects. Both groups have separate biweekly meetings. During these gatherings, everyone briefly reports on his or her work activities. Additionally, as a regular part of these meetings, one of the architects elaborates on what he or she is doing at that moment and which issues are being addressed. Concerns raised in such talks include, for example, the approach being used, the projected results, and also the fundamental choices that must be made. This is subsequently discussed in somewhat more detail. In this way, architects keep each other informed about what they are doing, and help each other out. Of course, they regularly consult with each other outside of these meetings, but this is often limited to contacts between the same people. The complete architecture team has monthly departmental meetings. These are mostly devoted to announcements from higher up, housekeeping items, important developments in the organization and sometimes a presentation by one of the architects.

At B-Sure Bank, clear steps have been taken in the architectural domain. Still, Arnold Hedges, the head of the Architecture department, is convinced that more can be gained from architecture – he is just not sure what or where. In order to substantiate his theory, he has decided to perform an Architectural Review to plot the situation at B-Sure Bank on the Quadrant Model. He provides the following responses to the Review's 12 statements:

*Table 5.2* **Architectural Review for B-Sure Bank**

| No. | Statement | Yes/No |
|---|---|---|
| 1 | In our organization, architecture is a part of the management agenda | Yes |
| 2 | A new version of our organization's architecture has been issued in recent years | Yes |
| 3 | Architects and business representatives are in regular contact with each other | Yes |
| 4 | I think that at least half of the architectural initiatives in our organization have a business sponsor | No |
| 5 | I know which director is responsible for architecture | Yes |
| 6 | Our architectural process is regularly evaluated | No |
| 7 | I think that at least a quarter of the organization has immediate access to the most recent version of the architecture | Yes |
| 8 | In our organization, architecture plays an important role in decisions about projects | No |
| 9 | An architect is involved in at least half of the projects at our organization | No |
| 10 | Our architects have a customer-focused attitude | Yes |
| 11 | Completion of a project is only acknowledged after an architectural review has been performed on the project | No |
| 12 | Non-compliance with architecture results at least in being asked to justify the non-compliance | No |

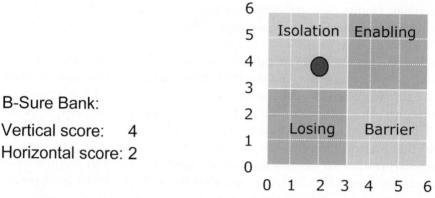

*Figure 5.7* **Position of B-Sure Bank in the Quadrant Model**

Translation of the answers into the Quadrant Model yields the diagram in Figure 5.7.

The level of architectural thinking is clearly better developed than is the integration of the architecture into the organization. This accords well with Arnold's intuition: the Strategic Dialogue occurs as it should, but the link with development could be better. He decides to devote a workshop to this subject, inviting a delegation of people involved in the change processes at B-Sure Bank. The directors, management, architects and developers will be represented. The objective is to determine if they agree with Arnold's analysis and to investigate the architectural processes somewhat more deeply. This is arranged, and the delegates meet on a Thursday morning. First of all, Arnold has everyone complete the Architectural Review with the 12 statements. The answers are then compared and, after some discussion, they unanimously adopt a view that confirms Arnold's.

Subsequently, the group is divided into three subgroups, and each is given a board with one of the DYA processes drawn on it. The task is to indicate how the relevant process is being conducted at B-Sure Bank, what is done well and what could be done better. The results are represented in Figures 5.8 through 5.10.

The common conclusion is that the relationship with projects is currently the weakest point in the architecture function. Projects must find their own way in the architecture domain. The relationship is strongly reactive and could be somewhat more proactive. Furthermore, they arrive at the conclusion that the mutual collaboration, alignment and exchange of knowledge could be better. The architecture board functions fairly well, but more use could be made of it. For instance, ideas for the development of architecture could be discussed by the architecture board at a much earlier stage.

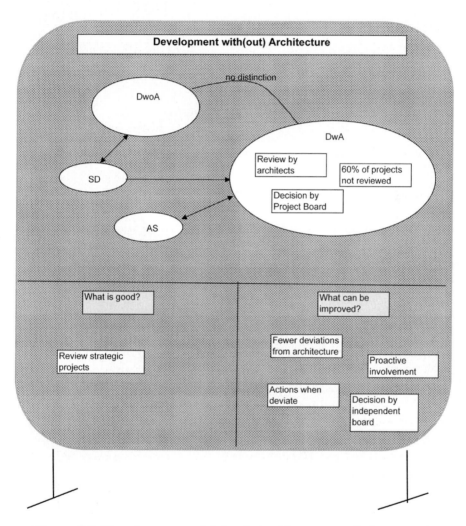

*Figure 5.8* **Development with(out) Architecture at B-Sure Bank**

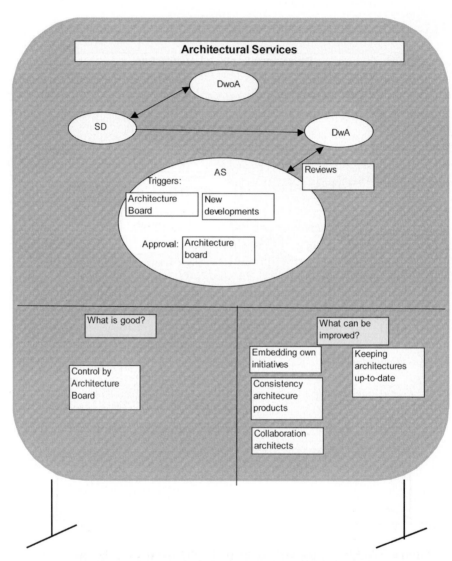

*Figure 5.9* **Architectural Services at B-Sure Bank**

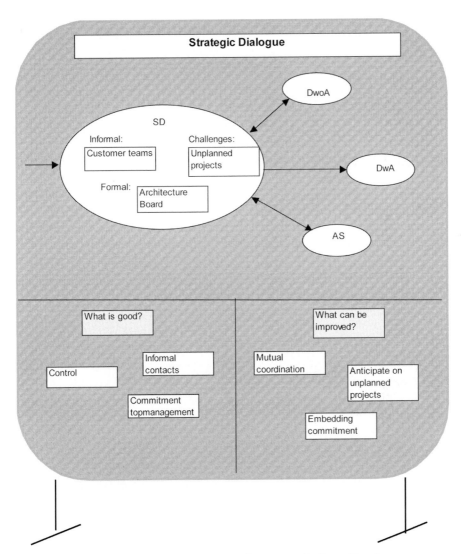

*Figure 5.10* **Strategic Dialogue at B-Sure Bank**

# 6 PRIORITIES IN THE ARCHITECTURAL PROCESS

The employment of architecture is a multifaceted process. To make the architecture function effectively, it is essential to set priorities. Not everything can be done at once, and fortunately this is not necessary. The Architecture Maturity Matrix helps guide the proper choices.

## 6.1 Crisis Situation at B-Sure Bank

"But what value does architecture add to the organization? I have some sympathy for the information analysts grumbling on this question. Three weeks ago, they asked about an architectural review, and we appeared not to take notice. How else should they react?" These were the words of Mary Bates, architect at B-Sure Bank.

"We just need more time," answered Kevin McAndrew. "Lately we've been busy working out the details of portfolio management and organizing issue management. They're just as important, since management is asking about them. We can't do everything at once."

" That's all very nice, but the projects just keep on churning along, don't they?" said John Hill, throwing his two cents in. "They're not going to wait until we get our act together. I completely agree with Mary! We have to make our added value as clear as day."

The architects at B-Sure Bank are in a crisis meeting. Rumblings of discontent about the quality and usefulness of the architecture team have been coming from various places in the organization. The team needs to take action to avoid losing its credibility. The workshop held a few weeks ago revealed that the organization had drifted into the isolation sector. The relationship with projects must be strengthened and internal collaboration is weak. At the same time, information managers continue to clamor for concrete results. There is so much to be done – but where to begin? Any ideas?

## 6.2  *Not Everything Can Happen at Once*

The Quadrant Model sheds some light on the position of architecture in the organization. Using the DYA Model, we gain insight into the functioning of the most important architectural processes. The architectural framework helps to map everything that is happening in the architectural domain. In brief, with the help of the above models, we can get a good snapshot of the current architecture function in an organization, including its strong and weak points. This snapshot helps us to understand why certain architectural items do not go as well as intended and why it is so difficult to deliver on all our promises.

Cultivating our understanding of the situation produces fertile ground on which to build. In many organizations, developing powerful, professional and effective architectural practices involves a prolonged process of trial and error. There are many reasons for this. Often, the level of ambition is too high: the architects are expected to do everything at once. They must establish an overall vision and corresponding architecture but, at the same time, they are constantly called to resolve very specific issues. It is important for them to be involved in all decision-making processes, to be informed about new developments and to participate in projects. The fact that the tasks and responsibilities of the architects are not always clear, often because the lion's share of the architecture function is still on the drawing board, does not make the situation any easier. If the architects also have to spend time building their own knowledge and skills, is it then any wonder that they sometimes can't see the forest for the trees? And we still have not mentioned the fact that the dialogue with business must, in the meantime, remain active.

In short, the architects run an enormous risk of, on the one hand, taking too much on and accomplishing nothing or, on the other hand, making snap judgments that may overlook a critical element. Either will give rise to the view that nothing useful comes from architecture, and could ultimately result in the organization abandoning it. At the same time, the architects feel that they are exhausting themselves running around in circles.

To define the architecture function in an effective manner, it is essential to set clear priorities and make appropriate choices. Precisely because architecture is an issue affecting the entire organization, it is impossible to address everything at once. The balance between thought and action, as represented by the two dimensions of the Quadrant Model, must be monitored, but making architecture effective typically involves finer distinctions. Based on our experiences with the architecture function, we have defined 18 key areas that need to be considered, sooner or later, in order for architecture to be effective.

## 6.3 Eighteen Key Areas of Architectural Maturity

We have broken down architectural practice into 18 areas that must be represented in performing the architecture function. Together, these 18 key areas elaborate the two dimensions of the Quadrant Model. In some cases, the emphasis is on the dimension involving the *level of architectural thinking*; in others, on *integration within the organization.*

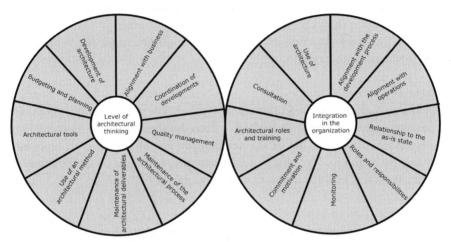

*Figure 6.1* **Eighteen key areas of architectural maturity**

*Development of architecture*
The development of architecture can be undertaken in various ways, varying from isolated, autonomous projects to an interactive process of continuous facilitation. In the first case, the emphasis is placed on architecture considered as a product, in the second, on architecture as a process. The more that architectural design is incorporated as a continuous process within an organization's trajectory of change, the greater is the chance that real value will be added.

*Use of architecture*
Developing architecture is not really an end in itself. Architecture has a goal: it must accomplish something; it needs to be put to use. In practice, the uses of architecture can vary. It may merely be a conduit for information, or it may be a means of governing individual projects or even a tool for managing the entire organization.

*Alignment with business*
Architecture is justified insofar as it supports and facilitates business goals. Alignment with business (the degree to which the architectural process is in tune with what the business wants and is capable of) is therefore very important.

*Alignment with the development process*
Architecture needs to channel changes in such a way that the business goals are achieved in the most effective manner. Alignment with the development process – the relation between the architectural process and development process – is therefore extremely important, no matter whether it involves process, organization or IT development. How is the development process synchronized with the overarching architectural process?

*Alignment with operations*
Architecture is not only important for development – the alignment with operations and maintenance (O&M) is also important. These elements work reciprocally: principles and guidelines that are important from an operations perspective have to be included in the architecture, and based on that architecture, parameters must be imposed on O&M activities.

*Relationship to the as-is state*
Architecture is frequently associated with a desired state of affairs: the so-called to-be state. Most organizations also have to deal with an existing situation based on historical growth (frequently without architecture). In assessing the suitability of the architecture, it is important to realize that a set of circumstances already exists, which has its own range of possibility and impossibility. If this relationship to the as-is state is ignored, there is a danger that the organization will be able to do little with its elegantly drafted scenarios for future architecture.

*Roles and responsibilities*
If the roles and responsibilities concerning architectural thinking and taking action are clearly and unambiguously outlined to everyone, discussions and differences of opinion about architecture are prevented from falling into limbo. Moreover, parties can then be questioned about their own specific contribution to architecture.

*Coordination of developments*
In an organization, a (large) number of developments take place in all sorts of areas at more or less the same time. Some of these developments are interrelated.

Architecture is the control instrument to make sure that the content of such developments is coordinated. Of course, architecture must then be employed for this purpose.

## Monitoring
It is generally insufficient to just state that projects must comply with the architecture. Without a control mechanism, the temptation will be too great to choose the path of least resistance and to ignore the architecture at certain points.

## Quality management
Obviously, the successful employment of the architecture depends upon its quality. The goal of quality management is to ensure such quality.

## Maintenance of the architectural process
Like every other process, the architectural process needs to be maintained. This is the only way to safeguard the effectiveness and efficiency of architecture. Maintenance of the architectural process means that a cycle of evaluation, development, improvement and implementation is periodically re-run.

## Maintenance of architectural deliverables
It is not enough to issue architectural products (such as standards, guidelines and models); they must also be maintained. Maintaining architectural deliverables means updates are provided and outdated products eliminated, as necessary. Active maintenance guarantees that the architecture is always current and fully functional.

## Commitment and motivation
Commitment and motivation by the architecture stakeholders is critical in bringing the architecture up to speed and making it successful. These stakeholders include not only the architects but also, and especially, senior business and IT management, plus project management. Business and IT management are primarily responsible for creating a favorable atmosphere. This ensures that the architectural process is given sufficient time, money and resources. Ideally, there is support for the architectural artifacts (architectural principles and models) at all levels of management.

## Architectural roles and training
Being an architect is demanding. Architects not only need to possess the skills to develop architectures, they also need to have the knowledge and understanding for process development, systems development and technical infrastructures. As

if that were not enough, high demands are made on their social and management skills. Acquiring this skill set takes training. Hence defining the architect's role and providing the necessary training is an important concern.

## Use of an architectural method

The way an organization develops its architecture is a methodical procedure made up of activities, techniques, tools and deliverables. This method must be sufficiently versatile and generic that it can be reused, but it also must be sufficiently particularized to be effective. If this method is made so generic that many components must be redeveloped each time it is employed, or if it is so detailed that it cannot be adapted for use in other situations, the architectural method is inefficient. Organizations should take care to maintain a balance in their method between specific detail and generic applicability.

## Consultation

A great deal of consultation with various stakeholders is required in developing architecture. Stakeholders like business managers, process owners, information managers, project managers and IT specialists are involved. These consultations are very important in making the architectural process function well. They make the architectural requirements clear and they create an opportunity to share the results of the architectural process with the users of the architecture (such as projects and operations).

## Architectural tools

Working with architecture can be aided by architectural tools. They should be well suited to their task. Using tools in an integrated manner, preferably with the support of a repository, maximizes their efficiency and effectiveness.

## Budgeting and planning

The development of architecture can be budgeted and planned. Careful budgeting and planning helps de-mystify architecture. It also shows the organization what it can expect. Budgeting and planning can range from drafting occasional plans to collecting past experiences with architecture.

We should not try to bring all 18 of these areas to the same level of perfection at the same time. Achieving uniform perfection all at the same time is impossible, but is also unnecessary. There is an art to making the right choices, maintaining the proper balance and raising the architecture function to a higher level one step at a time.

## 6.4　*Not Everything Must Happen at Once*

Each of the 18 factors in effective architectural practices must receive sufficient attention. This does not, however, mean that each must be given equal consideration at all times.

First of all, not every factor is equally relevant at the start. The use of architectural tools will certainly become a key concern at some point, but organizations that are still in the phase of building up architectural practice can focus more productively on the purpose of the architecture and its alignment with other processes. Tools will have their turn.

Furthermore, any given area need not be brought up to its full state of development right away. Different levels of maturity can be distinguished in each of the various areas. The development of architecture undergoes several growth stages. Often architecture is initially approached in a project-based manner, each project having a beginning and an end. At a higher level of maturity, the development of architecture is viewed as a continuous process: the architecture is never complete and must be constantly kept up to date. In the final stage, the development of architecture is ultimately viewed as a continuous facilitation process; it is fully focused on achieving the business goals.

As a result of this differentiated growth, each key area has its own path of development, distinguishable into meaningful levels. The nature and the number of levels in each path depend entirely on the character of the individual concern and are established independently of all the other concerns. As shown in Table 6.1, the path of development in most areas passes, in practice, through three levels. Two of the categories involve only two levels. In two others, it is useful to distinguish a fourth level. The levels identified in the following table are further elaborated in Appendix 1.

Distinguishing key areas, each having its own developmental path, makes it possible to implement and optimize architectural practices step by step. It provides guidance in giving the proper amount of attention to each area of concern at the proper time. Using it, the organization can take manageable measures for improvement in those areas offering the greatest added value in light of the as-is state of the organization. To do this, we must set the optimal course the organization should take to navigate through all the cells in Table 6.1. What level should we endeavor to attain in a particular area at any given time? The answer to this question is compiled in an Architecture Maturity Matrix.

## *Table 6.1* Maturity levels in each key area

| Key area | Level A | Level B | Level C | Level D |
|---|---|---|---|---|
| Development of architecture | Architecture undertaken in projects | Architecture as a continuous process | Architecture as a facilitation process | – |
| Use of architecture | Architecture used informatively | Architecture used to steer content | Architecture integrated into the organization | – |
| Alignment with business | Architecture tested for compatibility with business goals | Architectural process geared to business goals | Architectural process is an integral component of business | – |
| Alignment with the development process | Ad hoc | Structural | Interactive | – |
| Alignment with operations | Ad hoc | Structural | Interactive | – |
| Relationship to the as-is state | Attention to the as-is state | Attention to migration | – | – |
| Roles and responsibilities | Responsibility for architectural content assigned | Management responsible for the architectural process | Senior management responsible for the effect of architecture | – |
| Coordination of developments | Steering the content in each project | Coherence among projects | – | – |
| Monitoring | Reactive monitoring | Proactive monitoring | Embedded monitoring | Integrated monitoring |
| Quality management | Retrospective validation | Quality process developed | Embedded quality policy | – |
| Maintenance of the architectural process | Maintenance performed in a fragmented manner | Maintenance procedures are established | Continuous process improvement | – |
| Maintenance of architectural deliverables | Maintenance performed in a fragmented manner | Maintenance procedures are established | A maintenance policy exists | – |
| Commitment and motivation | Allocation of budget and time | Architecture integrated into processes of change | Continuous architectural improvement accepted by the organization | – |
| Architectural roles and training | Role recognized | Role described | Role supported | Role valued |
| Use of an architectural method | Project specific | Organization generic | Organizationally optimizing R&D activities | – |
| Consultation | Internal architectural meetings | Meetings with sponsors and users of architecture | All-encompassing discussions about the quality of the architectural processes in the organization | – |
| Architectural tools | Ad hoc and product based | Structural and process based | Integration of tools | – |
| Budgeting and planning | Project specific | Organization generic | Optimizing | – |

## 6.5 Using the Architecture Maturity Matrix to Set Priorities

There is a natural sequence to incorporating the various aspects involved in architectural practice. That is, the key areas and the levels into which they are differentiated can be approached in a specific order. Practice has taught us that it is generally advisable to take first steps toward level A in three areas: *development of architecture* (as architecture can only be incorporated into work if it first exists), *alignment with business* (to prevent, right from the start, architecture work from becoming cut off from business goals), and *commitment and motivation* (to secure the necessary support from management). Once a start has been made on these areas, then concentrate on obtaining "A" levels in the *use of architecture* (to make the aim and intention of the architectural practice clear), *alignment with the development process* (to ensure that the architecture is incorporated into projects), and *consultation* (to promote collaboration within the architecture team). In effect, the levels for all 18 key areas can be comparatively ranked in a similar manner. The resulting set of interdependencies is represented by the Architecture Maturity Matrix in Figure 6.2.

| Key area | Stage 0 | 1 | 2 | 3 | 4 | 5 | 6 | 7 | 8 | 9 | 10 | 11 | 12 | 13 |
|---|---|---|---|---|---|---|---|---|---|---|---|---|---|---|
| Development of architecture | | A | | | B | | | C | | | | | | |
| Use of architecture | | | A | | | B | | | | C | | | | |
| Alignment with business | | A | | | | B | | | | C | | | | |
| Alignment with the development process | | | A | | | | B | C | | | | | | |
| Alignment with operations | | | | | A | | B | | | C | | | | |
| Relationship to the as-is state | | | | | A | | | B | | | | | | |
| Roles and responsibilities | | | | A | B | | | | | C | | | | |
| Coordination of developments | | | | | | | A | | B | | | | | |
| Monitoring | | | | A | B | C | D | | | | | | | |
| Quality management | | | | | | | A | B | | | | C | | |
| Maintenance of the architectural process | | | | | | | A | B | | C | | | | |
| Maintenance of architectural deliverables | | | | | A | | B | | | | | C | | |
| Commitment and motivation | | A | | | | | B | C | | | | | | |
| Architectural roles and training | | | | A | B | | | C | | | D | | | |
| Use of an architectural method | | | | A | | | | | B | | | | | C |
| Consultation | | | A | B | | | | C | | | | | | |
| Architectural tools | | | | | | | A | | | B | | | | C |
| Budgeting and planning | | | | A | | | | | | B | | C | | |

*Figure 6.2* **Architecture Maturity Matrix**

The letters in the cells of the matrix stand for the levels of maturity in the various categories from Table 6.1. Reading the matrix from left to right shows the order and extent of progress to be made in each area. This goes as follows. In the column headed Stage 1, there are "A"s in three key areas (i.e. *development of architecture*, *alignment with business*, and *commitment and motivation*). This means that the minimum level (level A) must be attained in these three areas first. They are immediately followed in priority by the areas involving *use of architecture*, *alignment with the development process* and *consultation* (the "A"s in the Stage 2 column). And so on. Once the key areas marked with an "A" in column 3 have been brought to the "A" level, the *development of architecture* needs to be upgraded to the next level, the "B" level. This is indicated by the B that appears in column 4 for this key area. Concurrently, we are working to attain an initial "A" level in *alignment with operations*. And so on. The model therefore concretely indicates the order in which we can best work on the various key areas. In this way, it could very well be that one of the areas must first reach the highest level, while others are not yet at level A. An example of this is the relative positioning of the *development of architecture* (at level C in column 7) and *quality management* (only at level A in column 7).

In this way, it is possible to work one step at a time towards stage 13. However, this final stage represents a measure of perfection that not every organization wishes to attain. The principle "just enough, just in time" also applies to architectural practice. It is more sensible to set a lower stage as an initial target: for example, stage 3. Once this goal is achieved, the organization can then decide if this is sufficient, or if it wants to adopt a higher stage – perhaps stage 6 – as a new goal. In this process, it is possible to distinguish the following stages:

- *Stage 3*: a start is made on the employment of architecture. The most important key areas are developed to a basic level. There is an awareness that architecture must be embedded into the organization and work is being done on this matter.

- *Stage 6*: nearly all the key areas are developed to a basic level. Consideration is given to architecture as a process. Architectural practices are structurally established.

- *Stage 8*: architecture now facilitates the most important organizational changes. There is commitment throughout the organization.

- *Stage 10*: architecture is used as an integral part of all the changes occurring in an organization. Architectural practices are integral to the organization.

- *Stage 13*: architectural practices are at such a high level of proficiency that architectural processes and products are continuously optimized.

Our experience is that most organizations are still trying to attain stage 3 or have just reached that level. At that level, architecture has a reasonable profile. It produces some results, but things could be better. Organizations that have reached stage 6 will notice that their architecture function is substantially more effective. From this stage, it may be worth considering whether it makes any sense to continue to stage 8. Not every organization will choose to do so. Stage 8 will only yield additional returns if the organization is ready for it in other areas of structure and management.

There is, however, a preliminary step in setting goals and priorities: determining the current position of the organization with regard to the 18 key areas. The as-is state can be represented in the Maturity Matrix in the manner illustrated in Figure 6.3.

| Stage | 0 | 1 | 2 | 3 | 4 | 5 | 6 | 7 | 8 | 9 | 10 | 11 | 12 | 13 |
|---|---|---|---|---|---|---|---|---|---|---|---|---|---|---|
| Key area | | | | | | | | | | | | | | |
| Development of architecture | | A | | | B | | C | | | | | | | |
| Use of architecture | | | A | | B | | | C | | | | | | |
| Alignment with business | | A | | | B | | | C | | | | | | |
| Alignment with the development process | | | A | | | B | C | | | | | | | |
| Alignment with operations | | | | A | | B | | | C | | | | | |
| Relationship to the as-is state | | | | A | | | B | | | | | | | |
| Roles and responsibilities | | | A | | B | | | C | | | | | | |
| Coordination of developments | | | | | A | | | B | | | | | | |
| Monitoring | | | A | | B | C | D | | | | | | | |
| Quality management | | | | | | A | | B | | | C | | | |
| Maintenance of the architectural process | | | | | A | | B | | C | | | | | |
| Maintenance of architectural deliverables | | | A | | | B | | | | | C | | | |
| Commitment and motivation | | A | | | | B | C | | | | | | | |
| Architectural roles and training | | | A | | B | | C | | | | D | | | |
| Use of an architectural method | | | A | | | | | | B | | | | | C |
| Consultation | | | A | B | | | C | | | | | | | |
| Architectural tools | | | | | | A | | | | B | | | | C |
| Budgeting and planning | | | A | | | | | | | B | | C | | |

*Figure 6.3* **Architecture Maturity Matrix for an organization at stage 0**

The organization in Figure 6.3 is still at stage 0 because the area involving *alignment with business* has still not been developed at all. The matrix shows that the organization should focus on this area. Once the basic A level is reached here, the organization will have attained stage 2. *Monitoring* is then the area that it subsequently has to work on, in order to advance to stage 3. In this fashion, we can concretely map out a path of development.

A pension company has been working with architecture for some time but has the sense that architecture could do more than it currently does. There are nagging doubts about its general effectiveness. But where should improvements be made? Management decides to have an assessment done.

The assessors employ the Architecture Maturity Matrix. They begin by interviewing stakeholders from all parts of the organization. The results from these interviews are translated for use with the Maturity Matrix. At first, this is not very successful. Something appears not to fit, until they realize that two architectural "worlds" exist in the organization. One division is entering a new world migrating their applications to a new architecture, and the rest of the organization is back in the old world continuing the use of the old operational applications without any thought to architecture. The assessors decide to make two matrices, at which point everything falls into place. The new world turns out to be at stage 2, while the old world is still at stage 0. A big gulf exists between the old and new worlds. These results lead, among other things, to the understanding that the old world must certainly be included in the process of change. Otherwise the new developments will find no connection with the rest of the organization. Although the new world may take the lead, the gap must not become too large. Based on the matrices, they decide to make an effort to bring the new world up to stage 3 and the old world up to stage 2.

## 6.6 Targeted Action

Employing architecture involves many factors. We have defined 18 of them, each one with its own developmental path. That is too many to attend to all at once, so we use the Maturity Matrix to bring things into focus. By representing the organization on this matrix, we can determine the key areas that must be emphasized in the near future and the extent to which this needs to be done. On this basis we can plan targeted improvements.

For those who wish to make use of the matrix, Appendix 1 provides more detailed information. To establish where an organization stands, each area of concern has a number of checkpoints at every level. Using these checkpoints, it is possible to determine whether the organization has attained the appropriate level. If the organization does not fulfill all the checkpoints of a level, but nevertheless wants to use the Maturity Matrix to reach that level, appropriate actions can be mapped out. These actions are, in part, derived from the checkpoints. At the same time, the actions must always suit the organization's circumstances. Formulating improvements should never be a purely mechanical process.

Based on our experiences, we have included in the Appendix a number of possible improvement activities for each level. These can help to achieve the level in question. The activities are explicitly intended as examples and are neither exhaustive nor applicable to every situation. They are meant to be sources of inspiration – extract whatever is useful and then supplement them with your own activities.

## 6.7 Prioritizing B-Sure Bank

The results of the workshop involving the architects, directors, management and developers, plus the negative rumblings coming from the organization, led Arnold Hedges to a decision. To better integrate architecture within B-Sure Bank, he decided to initiate a structured professionalization program. The first step was to determine B-Sure Bank's position in the Maturity Matrix. Testing on all checkpoints yielded the diagram in Figure 6.4.

| Stage | 0 | 1 | 2 | 3 | 4 | 5 | 6 | 7 | 8 | 9 | 10 | 11 | 12 | 13 |
|---|---|---|---|---|---|---|---|---|---|---|---|---|---|---|
| Key area |
| Development of architecture | | A | | | B | | | C | | | | | | |
| Use of architecture | | | A | | | B | | | | C | | | | |
| Alignment with business | | A | | | | B | | | | C | | | | |
| Alignment with the development process | | | A | | | | B | C | | | | | | |
| Alignment with operations | | | | | A | | | B | | | C | | | |
| Relationship to the as-is state | | | | | A | | | | B | | | | | |
| Roles and responsibilities | | | | A | B | | | | | | C | | | |
| Coordination of developments | | | | | | | A | | | B | | | | |
| Monitoring | | | | A | B | | C | D | | | | | | |
| Quality management | | | | | | | A | | | B | | | C | |
| Maintenance of the architectural process | | | | | | | A | B | C | | | | | |
| Maintenance of architectural deliverables | | | | A | | | | B | | | | | C | |
| Commitment and motivation | | A | | | | | B | C | | | | | | |
| Architectural roles and training | | | | A | B | | | C | | | | D | | |
| Use of an architectural method | | | | A | | | | | | B | | | | C |
| Consultation | | | A | | B | | | C | | | | | | |
| Architectural tools | | | | | | | A | | | | B | | | C |
| Budgeting and planning | | | | A | | | | | | | B | C | | |

**Figure 6.4 Maturity Matrix for B-Sure Bank**

The matrix revealed that B-Sure Bank was at stage 1. *Alignment with the development process* and *consultation* would be the immediate areas to address. *Monitoring* would be next. These findings agreed with the conclusions that the team had drawn from analyzing its own processes using the DYA Model. There was a need for a more proactive engagement with projects and for better mutual collaboration. Insofar as *monitoring* was concerned, project deliverables were being reviewed. But, in the end, projects only complied with the architecture sporadically. Consequently, there were things to be improved in that respect as well.

Arnold Hedges decided to only focus on these three key areas in the near future. He was certain that if he could improve the relationship with projects and make it as good as the relationship with divisions, he would advance the effectiveness of architecture. This entailed collaboration in projects right from the start, instead of only retrospective testing. He had better go and visit the two most important project managers at B-Sure Bank.

In addition, he would reinvigorate the discussion at the architecture board about the importance of architecture in steering projects. Management certainly wanted such control, but seemed always to make short-term concessions.

Finally, he also wanted to do something about the architect meeting. As things now stood, it was more or less dormant. A set agenda was routinely worked through, but no one was really interested in it. However, the workshop had been a great success. And the need to collaborate and share knowledge was evident. He had to try to give more substance to the meetings and to ensure that something came out of them. Consequently, they had to be less informal than they had been up to now.

# 7 THE ARCHITECT AS A SUCCESS FACTOR

The architect is an important factor in the successful employment of architecture. His or her customer orientation, expertise, empathy and readiness to work and share knowledge with others all contribute to this success.

## 7.1 A Good Architecture Poorly Received

Fred Brooks was clearly fed up when he told his story to his fellow architect, Anne Moreland. "You know I have developed an application architecture for the shared service center at Mortgages. It's o.k., isn't it? Why then, did I get torn apart by management when I presented it to them? They asked me where on earth I got the idea to propose such a thing. But, you must agree it is a good architecture. All the processes are described, it has a data model that includes all the factors involved in the back office at Mortgages, and the application architecture has been developed in total compliance with the guidelines of our service architecture. In terms of content, they couldn't actually punch any holes in it. In fact, we never got around to content. There was immediate hostility. Where did I go wrong?"

Anne was sympathetic. Fred was a good professional with years of experience as an architect, and he knew all about mortgages. He was perhaps somewhat of a loner, but very knowledgeable. Anne thought about it a moment and then asked Fred, "What approach did you take?"

Fred replied, "Because I know all the processes involved in mortgages, I was able to come up with a process model quickly. I circulated it for review, but everyone thought it was fine. And I had expected as much – it wouldn't be very good if I didn't know these processes by now! Subsequently, I set up a data model and, with the aid of a CRUD matrix, I drafted the application architecture. It all took less than three months. Nice and fast, wasn't it?"

Anne could not deny this, but something certainly had gone wrong. She asked, "Who was the sponsor and who else did you involve in the project?"

"Arnold Hedges was my sponsor," Fred stated. "He asked me three months ago to develop this architecture, and suggested that there was some urgency. Consequently, I didn't involve too many others. Particularly since I had already circulated the process model."

Things gradually became clear to Anne. Finally she asked Fred, "And did you know what management wanted to accomplish with the application architecture?"

"Well, to my mind, they just wanted to get their hands on the desired application architecture as quickly as possible. But then, I don't understand why they reacted as they did," was Fred's reply.

"Mmm," Anne responded. "You know, there is a big difference between delivering a good product and getting that good product accepted. I also had to learn this the hard way. But I think management, because they weren't involved in the development, had a sort of knee-jerk reaction. For them, you were a guy with a lot of nerve telling them what choices *they* had to make concerning *their* applications. You would feel the same if, all of a sudden, someone with a new approach to architecture came along and said that you had to immediately use it because it did everything better. These sorts of reactions can be avoided by involving people in the process right from the start. What I usually do is …"

## 7.2  The Architect in the Effective Employment of Architecture

In optimizing and professionalizing architectural practices, it is not just the content and the process that is important, but also the architect. (By *architect*, we mean the enterprise, business, information or IT architect.) The architect personifies an organization's entire process of working with architecture, and the architect can, certainly at the early stages, make or break the success of this process. The manner in which the architect fulfills his or her role has a great deal of influence on whether the process secures acceptance and support. An architect who operates inside an ivory tower enjoys less support, as a rule, than an architect who is immersed in the organization, has a network and knows the organization's needs.

An organization in the telecommunications sector has recently set up the architecture role in the Planning and Strategy department. Three architects have been appointed and given the assignment of putting IT changes on the right course. In the past, too much uncontrolled growth had occurred, which had to be checked. In practice, the architects help to devise alternative ways of realizing the business goal, offer their recommendations about which alternatives are the best and then assist in estimating the time and money required. Architectural principles are present to a limited extent and have particular relevance to interfacing. The roles and responsibilities of the architects have not yet been crystallized.

During the execution of the SWOT analysis, it became evident that the architect's working procedures were strongly person-related. One architect focuses on supporting projects. He helps to find the best solution. Project managers are eager to make use of his services. Another architect sees himself much more as the developer of the architectural principles to which projects must conform. Such an attitude does not sit well with the project managers. They feel that this architect elevates architecture into a goal rather than an aid for projects. In their eyes, the second architect is not performing well, and they prefer not to involve him in their projects.

This practical situation, as described, illustrates the problems organizations wrestle with in beginning to employ architecture. How well the architecture is accepted depends upon how well the architects serve projects. But wait – was architecture not created precisely to restrain the uncontrolled proliferation caused by allowing the short-term interests of projects to prevail?

In a situation like this, it is extremely important for project managers to understand that there may be a tension between project goals and enterprise goals. It's not only the project manager who must understand this - the architect must as well. He or she needs to understand that organizational interests can conflict with project interests. He must find a balance between forcing projects to comply with architecture and supporting projects in making the right choices within the architectural constraints.

## 7.3 Pitfalls and Tips for the Architect

Practice has shown that the role of the architect is especially challenging. This goes for both organizations that are just beginning to make use of architecture and organizations that have been employing it for a long time.

In organizations just beginning to work with architecture, the challenge for architects is to prove their added value – that is to say, their right to exist. Architecture has not yet been accepted as a business function. Experience shows that this is an enormous challenge. The architects are appointed at the moment when the organization is in urgent need of an architecture. Consequently, the architect is under a great deal of pressure to supply a good product. At the same time, architects are expected to involve the right stakeholders in the right manner. They must be able to disperse the architecture throughout the organization and ensure that projects are able to work with it. Not every architect is able to handle this task. Some become completely preoccupied with content and, in fact, too deeply submerged in it. Others try to clarify their role first and forget that they need to do something about content. The challenge for novice architects is to demonstrate how their work benefits the organization. Acceptance in projects is therefore of great importance.

In organizations where architecture has become an indispensable business function, the primary challenge for architects is to ensure that they continue to add value to the organization. These are often large organizations in which architecture has already proven itself. Dozens of architects work diligently at various levels and in various domains or areas. Architectural processes and approaches are standardized. Roles, tasks and responsibilities are clear. Yet experienced architects also turn out to have their blind spots. Some of them get completely lost in content: they work out all the fine points in their domain architectures, until there is no one who can understand them. Still others have accumulated so much knowledge about a certain domain that they forget to involve the stakeholders in the development of an architecture. Therefore, the experienced architect must, first of all, take care to stay in touch with the organization.

What makes somebody a good architect? What prevents a good business analyst, information analyst or IT specialist from automatically being a good architect? Over the years, our experiences have alerted us to a number of pitfalls into which both novices and experienced architects may fall. These hazards may cause the architect and any associated architecture to be accepted with difficulty, if at all. Becoming aware of these problems and avoiding them substantially increases the chance of gaining support and acceptance.

A frequent mistake architects make is thinking from the inside out. Experienced architects are especially prone to this. They know so much about certain areas that they regard themselves as more than capable of developing the architecture in these areas. They think they do not need to involve any stakeholders or sponsors – they would rather work on the basis of their own knowledge and experience. The risk here is that the results will not be accepted by the organization. The architecture is created too much as an end in itself.

Another pitfall, previously mentioned, is that architects may become completely submerged in content. They research the minutest details and design elaborate models. The architecture is only issued when, in their eyes, it is perfect. In cases like this it takes forever before architects show any results.

A novice architect is given the assignment of compiling an inventory of existing applications and modeling these applications and the interfaces among them. The point of the exercise is to quickly gather an initial impression about the extent to which applications are interlinked. The assignment is expected to take a month.

The architect visits various departments in order to extract the necessary information about each application. When the month is nearly over, the task is far from completed. The architect is still waiting for information from the departments. He is unable to answer questions about how long things are going to take. After all, that depends on the departments.

Later, it becomes apparent that he wanted to know nearly everything about an application there was to know and was only planning to construct the model when he had received all the information.

Frequently, the architect expects that, once his or her architecture is finished, it will also be used as the basis for projects. This is not a foregone conclusion. In practice, project members often don't even know that there is an architecture. Even if they do know of the architecture they may still not use it because they find it too "difficult," "abstract" or "cumbersome."

A large bank has been working with architecture for years. At this bank, an architect and an information analyst from the same IT service provider are assigned to the architecture department and to a large project respectively. The architect and the information analyst meet each other in a course. At that time, it becomes apparent that the information analyst is totally unaware that the bank even has any architecture, let alone an architecture department. He had never noticed or heard anything about it in his projects. The architect from the IT service provider was dumbfounded when he heard this.

Frequently architects want to initiate changes on their own. They begin a program or project in order to achieve a certain goal. In particular, technical architects tend to start projects based on technical architecture in order to realize (a part of) this architecture. The risk in this is that the architect may assume the sponsor's role. The realization of the architecture is then regarded as an end in itself, while the organization feels no need for it at all.

One last pitfall regularly occurs when architects do not clearly, or at all, explain the value they bring to their organizations. An architect plays an important role, but that may not be clear to others in the organization who do not appreciate its value. Whenever architects either offer or are asked to briefly explain what they do and why, it proves very difficult for them. The danger here is that they will be undervalued or they may be less in demand than architects who can explain things better.

The fact that these are frequent difficulties has a lot to do with the maturity of the architectural discipline. It is a relatively young area and it will take time for people to become accustomed to it. For architects, it is primarily a quest for the proper balance between the things that they do and the things that they must take into account: a balance between forcing projects to comply with architecture and supporting projects in a helpful manner, between the organization-wide interest and the interest of the individual stakeholder, between the development of abstract concepts and the ability to furnish concrete answers, between recording quick results and garnering support for these results, between uncertainty as to whether an architecture is practical and feasible and the construction and propagation of this architecture with full conviction, between speed and coherence.

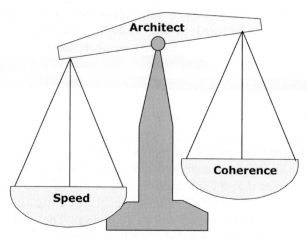

*Figure 7.1* **Finding the balance as an architect**

Being alert to the dangers and searching for the appropriate balance is, on the one hand, a question of experience. By doing, the architect learns to avoid the problems and to find the proper balance. On the other hand, there are a number of instruments that can help. In our daily practices, we have used them with great success.

*A good process*
If an architectural process has, to a reasonable extent, been implemented and accepted by the organization, the architect's role is clear to both the organization and the architect. The more widely accepted the process, the better the architect is able to function. In a good architectural process, the roles and responsibilities are clear. This is not only the case for the architects but also, for example, for the business management, IT management and project management involved with architecture. Such clarity prevents the architecture from being created in isolation and becoming regarded as an end in itself. Chapter 6 revealed the elements that

play a role in the improvement of the architectural process.

*Choose customer-focused architects, especially for the start-up phase*

In a relatively immature organization without a clear architectural process, there are a number of heroes who make the difference: architects who are well established in the organization have a great deal of goodwill and can play an important role in the acceptance of architectural practices. The more professional the architecture function becomes, the less important the individual architect. Therefore in establishing the architecture function in an organization, it is advisable to choose architects who are very committed to the organization, find it easy to build up a network and work in a customer-focused manner.

*Personal coaching*

Personal coaching or mentoring is an effective means of making an architect aware of the pitfalls into which one can fall. By engaging in bilateral talks, a trust relationship can be built up between architect and coach. Having these discussions regularly (for example, weekly), gives the architect active assistance to avoid future pitfalls.

*Peer review*

A peer review is a review of an architectural product by fellow architects. In this practice, the knife always cuts two ways. First, the quality of the product is increased. Second, knowledge is shared, since architects acquire knowledge of domains or areas other than the ones in which they work.

*Architect meeting*

In their practice, architects regularly have to deal with problems. These can vary from seeking a solution to a content problem to addressing a process-related issue like "whom should I involve, and in what?" Organizing periodic architect meetings offers the possibility of discussing these issues. The goal of such meetings is twofold: primarily, to learn something from each other, but also to develop a collective sensibility: you are not on your own. It is more effective to discuss a problem or issue with another than to sit brooding about it for days or weeks. Certainly in the start-up phase of an architecture team, it is advisable to hold an architect meeting weekly.

*Workshops*

Workshops are meetings focused on achieving a specific goal. Workshops for architects could have several possible goals: developing a collective frame of reference, exchanging best practices in diverse areas, training architects, rehearsing communications or creating mutual understanding among the architects. Workshops are an exceptional manner of sharing knowledge and awareness. They help the architect to find the right balance.

### Intervision

Architects are professionals who are regularly confronted by complex issues in which their own personal practices can also be part of the problem. Intervision is a means of presenting these issues to a group of architects from inside (or possibly outside) the organization and asking their opinions. Because intervision can also be relevant to the personal practices of the person submitting the issue, strict confidentiality is an important component of intervision. Intervision is also an excellent tool when architects are confronted with pitfalls – particularly the dangers of getting lost in content and working without a sponsor. It is sometimes striking to note that architects are very good at warning others about the pitfalls into which they themselves regularly fall.

### Working in pairs

Working in pairs is extremely well suited to the sharing of knowledge. Two heads are better than one – besides, it is an effective way of staying on course. In a pair, each has a duty to the other to honor their agreements. There will also be less time spent brooding over difficult problems – discussing it with the other partner brings a fresh perspective and often a swift resolution. Working in pairs is also a good way for less experienced architects to profit by being paired with more experienced ones.

### Training

Above all, acquiring expertise as an architect is a question of practical experience. On-the-job training is therefore the best way to learn. This can occur by pairing a novice with an experienced architect and having them execute an architectural project together. A second method is to assign an experienced architect to coach or mentor a novice. Taking training courses (e.g. on architectural modeling techniques) is another possible way of learning the architectural discipline. Formal training is sensible when the architect has been working in the discipline for some time, under supervision. Better than anyone, it is an experienced coach who can recognize the manner in which a particular architect can best increase his or her knowledge and skills.

An organization in the amusement industry has instituted a project they call "Implementing Architectural Practice," and Walter is coaching the project's architects. Walter's intention is to supervise the architects so that they learn to fulfill their roles well. Walter's goal and method is outlined in a general coaching plan.

Additionally, a personal coaching plan has been drafted for each individual architect. It contains the personal objectives of each individual. The table below displays the personal objectives of Gene, one of the three architects. Before being appointed as an architect, he had worked as an application manager.

*Table 7.1* **Sample coaching plan**

| Objective | Information | Intended result |
|---|---|---|
| Clarify my own role in the departmental context. | The role of the architect has not (yet) been finalized. The question: is the manner in which I fulfill my role the right one, and how does this role relate to those of my fellow architects? | Description of my own role. |
| Take more initiatives. | In general, initiative is a competence that an architect should have. Gene comes across as cautious. First, the conditions must be well defined and it must be crystal clear what is expected of him. An architect must, however, be ready to define the conditions when these are unclear. | Gene ensures that he is involved in projects and meetings where he can exercise influence. For projects or assignments in which he participates, Gene describes the approach: task, activities, deliverables and planning. |
| Be capable of abstraction and dare to communicate abstract concepts. | An architect must be capable of making decisions on a relatively abstract level. It is not necessary or sensible to work out issues in detail. Gene is someone who wants to elaborate things thoroughly and in detail. | Venture to reveal his ideas and concepts sooner, ask for feedback about them and apply it. Here, we are going to use a three-step approach in terms of testing and asking for feedback: |

| *Objective* | *Information* | *Intended result* |
|---|---|---|
| | He only reveals the fruits of his labour when it is absolutely necessary. Gene has acknowledged his difficulty with the communication of his ideas. How do you communicate a proposal? How do you win acceptance for it? How do others react to it? When you communicate, must the content be finalized, or can you send out your message earlier? Why do others not understand me? Gene implicitly assumes that something must be accepted when he, in performing his role as architect, says that it should. Gene sometimes does not understand why others do not understand him. | 1. feedback from coach,<br><br>2. feedback from fellow architects,<br><br>3. feedback from sponsor. |

## 7.4  Position of the Architect in the Organization

Employing architecture successfully depends not only on the role of the architect but his or her position in the organization, too. The position of the architect in the organization determines the associated controls on the architect's activities. If architects are placed in the wrong part of the organization with inadequate controls, it is difficult for them to adequately fulfill their roles. Such is the case, for example, when an architect is a member of a project team in which the project leader is also the sponsor. The project leader can then assign the architect the task of devising a solution that suits the parameters of time and money for the project. However, this is not always the best solution for the organization, so it is important to clarify the position of the architect. In this example, the project leader wants the architect to produce a solution within the limits of time and money set by the project. If the architect also bears other responsibilities and must serve more than one master, conflict becomes inevitable, and at that point there is no easy solution. It is best to clearly describe the architect's roles and responsibilities at the earliest possible stage.

Constructing a responsibility matrix provides an instrument for doing exactly that. In such a matrix, architecture-related tasks are mapped against the various roles and functions in the organization. The individual responsible and the person performing the task can subsequently be identified. Techniques used very frequently to clarify responsibilities are RACI and RAEW. The letters in RACI stand for:

— (R) Responsible: the individual delivering the end result.

— (A) Accountable: the person bearing the ultimate responsibility for the result.

— (C) Consulting: the persons providing input to reach the result.

— (I) Informed: the individuals informed about the result.

In RAEW, the letters stand for:

— (R) Responsibility: the individual delivering the end result.

— (A) Authority: the person checking and approving the result.

— (E) Expertise: the individuals giving advice based on certain expertise.

— (W) Work: the persons collaborating in producing the result.

Using a table, a care institution mapped the stakeholders involved in architecture against the relevant products. In this institution, the initiative to employ architecture originated in the IT strategy department. The table was drafted after a year of working with architecture, at a moment when business was beginning to come onside. The table identifies the stakeholders and indicates the manner in which they are involved in maintaining the various architectural products. They are involved in development and management of the architectural products, as well as in supervising their use.

### *Table 7.2* Sample RAEW matrix for a care institution

| | Project independent | | | Project dependent | | |
|---|---|---|---|---|---|---|
| | Architecture handbook | Communication plan | Enterprise architecture | Guidelines and Domain architecture | Business case | Project-start architecture |
| Architecture board | A | A | A | A | | |
| Management | | | | | A | |
| Patient representative | | | W/E | W/E | W/E | |
| Educational representative | | | W/E | W/E | W/E | |
| Representative for research | | | W/E | W/E | W/E | |
| Architectural community | E | | E | E | | |
| Process owner | | | E | E | R | E |
| Project leader | | | | | | R |
| Architect | W/E | W/E | W/E | W/E | W/E | W/E |
| Lead architect | R | R | R | R | | A |
| Information analyst and software engineer | | | | | | W |
| Application and technical manager | | | | E | | W |
| IT coordinator | | | | E | W | |

In clarifying roles and responsibilities, the sponsor's needs is an important element. In our view, an architect works in an organization for a sponsor. The sponsor is the person or body wishing to achieve a certain business goal. To realize this goal, it is necessary to have some insight into the required changes involving business, information, applications and technical infrastructure. It is the task of the architect to make these changes understandable and to guide their implementation. This is accomplished by developing principles and models for the mentioned domains (mostly in the form of domain architecture). Of course, as we stated in Chapter 4, it is important to consider the scope of the architecture, which aspects need to be described, in what form and to what depth.

If the business goal must be realized in program or project form, projects are the responsibility of a project manager. It is the task of the project manager to deliver a solution within the parameters of the architecture. The architect provides the project manager with principles and models (in the form of a project-start architecture). If the project manager believes that the project cannot comply with the architecture and still be accomplished within the designated time and budget, the sponsor must decide whether to deviate from the architecture or allocate more time and money.

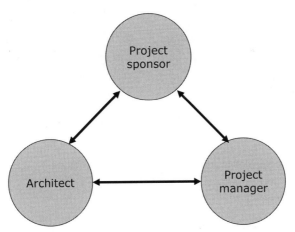

*Figure 7.2* **Position of the architect**

In the model shown in Figure 7.2, the sponsor plays an important role. Within the context of the business goal, the sponsor needs to weigh the relative importance of time, money and content, then make a decision. But a sponsor's decision will be complicated by the fact that within any organization there are several business goals in play at the same time. To establish some coherence among these goals, to make the necessary choices and to set priorities, an architecture board could be created. In fact, each of the roles of sponsor, architect and project manager needs to have some sort of support from, respectively, business management, architecture management and program management. These management groups are each represented on the architecture board, which also has a representative from senior management, as illustrated in Figure 7.3. An architecture board is a platform for content coherence and refinement.

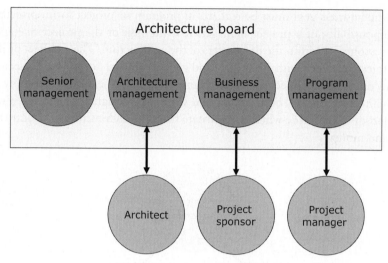

*Figure 7.3* **Architecture board**

The most prominent tasks of an architecture board are:

— assigning architectural tasks,

— formally approving architectural products,

— resolving architectural conflicts.

## 7.5 Place of the Architectural Team in the Organization

The organizational position of the architecture team or the architecture department has a number of variants in practice. Figure 7.4 illustrates a number of the most common variants.

In the model at the top left (1), architecture is nested within the IT department. This is often the case in organizations that are beginning to employ architecture. It is the IT department that introduces architectural practices into the organization and appoints IT architects. The purpose of employing architecture is often to standardize IT. The advantage of this model is that the architecture function can take root in the IT department, but the great disadvantage is that it becomes very difficult to win the business over to architectural thinking. Architecture is regarded as only relevant to IT.

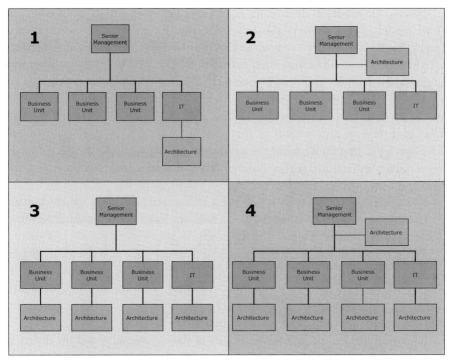

*Figure 7.4* **Place of architecture in the organization**

In the top right model (2), the architecture function is housed in a department accountable to senior management. This variant occurs sporadically, specifically in organizations in which senior management sees the importance of architecture right from the start and positions it directly over IT and business. The advantage of this model is the independence and the possibility of collaboration between business and IT. The disadvantage is the danger of the ivory-tower effect because architecture is separate from the business units and the IT department.

The model in the bottom left (3) illustrates a decentralized architecture function. Each business unit and the IT department has a separate little club of architects. This variant occurs in strongly decentralized organizations in which the business units are, to a large degree, autonomous. The advantage of this variant is that the architects are strongly involved, but the risk exists that they may devise solutions well suited to the business unit and the IT department but less than ideal for the organization in general. Moreover, there is a risk that business and IT architects may not collaborate well.

Finally, the model in the bottom right (4) is a combination of the second and third models. Here, there is also an architecture function at the organizational level. This variant occurs in organizations that are looking for a balance between activities best centralized and other activities that may be best left to the various organizational units. The central architects can, for example, be responsible for an organization's enterprise architecture while the architects in the decentralized units can look after the domain architectures and project-start architectures. The advantage of this variant is that shared items can be distinguished and developed once and for all, while the autonomy and dynamism of the decentralized departments remains intact. The disadvantage is that time is required to coordinate the central and decentralized architects.

There are organizations in which the architectural role is recognized but not developed into a team or department. In fact, the same concerns outlined above apply to such informal architecture functions.

Which model is best suited to a particular situation depends on various factors, such as the size of the organization, the architectural goal, the importance of information and IT for the organization, the degree of autonomy in the business units, the maturity with which change is handled, the culture of the organization and the acceptance of the architecture function.

The most significant factors are the size of the organization and the degree of autonomy in the business units. If we plot these factors against the models, we end up with the diagram in Figure 7.5.

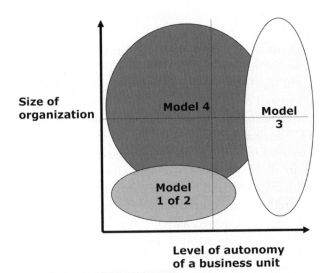

*Figure 7.5* **Positioning of the architecture function in the organization**

Models 1 and 2 are best suited to a small organization. The choice between models 1 or 2 depends on the strategic importance that IT has for the business. If IT plays a critical or central role (as in the case of an internet provider), then Strategic Dialogue between business and IT is crucial, and consequently model 2 is preferable. If IT instead plays a supporting role for business decisions, model 1 can be effective. An example of this second scenario is a production company in which IT does, in fact, support the business processes but is not decisive for the business model. In such a case, the primary goal of architecture is often standardization, which can certainly be accomplished from inside an IT department.

In larger organizations (e.g. holding companies) that consist of autonomous subsidiaries among which there is little or no interrelation, it is advisable to choose model 3. In this model, the architecture function is located only at the decentralized level. The reason for this is that little or no synergy among the subsidiaries is possible. Often the subsidiaries in such a situation have their own IT departments. The central IT department is then nothing more than a sort of internal IT supplier without any say in the IT choices of the subsidiaries.

Larger organizations that do have interrelated business units are best suited to model 4. This model makes it possible to establish for each level what is and is not generic at that level. Generic elements are assembled into the architecture function for that level. More specific items are left to the next underlying level.

## 7.6 Ensuring the Success of the Architect

The architect plays an important role in gaining acceptance and support for architectural practices. Success is determined by both the nature of the architect's role and its integration within the organization. Thinking from outside in is the best way to ensure this success and to add value to the organization. By taking the viewpoint of a sponsor or other stakeholder, an architecture can be built that actually helps the sponsor achieve business goals more efficiently and effectively. At the same time, the architect must perform a balancing act – constantly seeking the right balance between speed and coherence.

The following ten "rules to live by" enhance the architect's success:

1. Always find a sponsor for everything you do.

2. Know your stakeholders and their interests.

3. Work consciously on support and acceptance for your architecture.

4. Know what the organization wants.

5. Be observant; keep your eyes and your ears open.

6. Your architecture is not sacred, but the business goal is.

7. Share your knowledge with others.

8. Dare to present your provisional results.

9. Discuss problems with others.

10. Strive for coherence but do not forget speed.

## 7.7 The One-Day Retreat for B-Sure Bank Architects

The architecture department at B-Sure Bank has just had a one-day retreat. This day was scheduled because of the problems involving the performances of the architects in the organization that Arnold Hedges had come to hear about. In particular, business management had complained that the architects were listening to them too little and doing too much on their own.

The purpose of the retreat was to make the architects more aware of their function in the organization and to collectively explore activities that would lead to better integration with the organization.

To prepare for the retreat, Arnold conducted some research among business and IT management. He presented the conclusions from his research to the architects at the day-long retreat.

— *We are thinking too much from the inside out.* Instead of listening to our sponsors, we think we know better ourselves. Our sponsors do not accept that.

— *We are too slow.* That is how business sees us. When there is a good business idea, we first present all sorts of objections why its implementation would be so difficult, and then we take a lot of time to investigate what has to be changed.

— *We have a great deal of knowledge and are respected.* Business values and respects the knowledge that we have of their processes and systems. They understand that we are an indispensable resource when facing complex changes. Usually, we can put our finger on the sore spot relatively quickly.

These findings were discussed during the retreat, ultimately leading to the following understanding:

— *We want a more clearly defined sponsorship.* It seems that, in numerous architectural assignments, it is not really clear who the sponsor is. This leads architects to decide for themselves what they will do and when they will do it. If a presentation is then made of the results, it sometimes comes across as a surprise. We expect that when it is clear who the sponsor is for an architectural job at B-Sure Bank, we can come to clear agreement on issues such as stakeholders, deliverables and planning.

— *We must work in a more customer-focused manner.* Our customers, specifically business and IT management, see us as being too internally focused. This makes sense because we are still a young department that must first discover its role and how architecture can best be used at B-Sure Bank. But we are somewhat riddled with this tendency. We only issue results when they are completely finished and perfect. Working in a more customer-focused manner means that we should listen better to our sponsors and the stakeholders involved in architecture. In particular, we must keep an eye on their deadlines. This also means that we must actively involve these parties in our architectural work: for example, in workshops. We have to develop as architects into directors of a conceptual process rather than be individuals who work in isolation.

On the basis of this improved understanding, the following concrete actions have been adopted:

— Organizing a workshop with the sponsors of architecture. The goal of this workshop is to investigate how sponsors and other stakeholders can be involved in the development of architecture.

— Including the heading "sponsor" in the architectural assignment form. Arnold Hedges will only approve an architectural assignment when there actually is a sponsor whose name has been filled in. The architects still have the opportunity to tackle a problem proactively, but a sponsor for the activity must be found in all cases.

— Introducing the *intervision* instrument to make architects more aware of working in a customer-focused manner. It has been agreed that a pilot intervision group of five architects will be formed. The group will meet twice a month, at which time an architect will present his or her assignment to the others. Under the guidance of an experienced intervision moderator, there will be subsequent discussion of the extent to which the assignment is being performed in a customer-focused manner. Additionally, other problems that the architects encounter in their assignments will be discussed.

After three months, the pilot will be evaluated. The intervision group will assess what benefit intervision has provided. Based on this assessment, a decision will be made about wider implementation of intervision.

—   Undertaking the next few architectural assignments in pairs. Agreements will be made as to who does what in each assignment. It is understood that problems and dilemmas are to be discussed directly with the working partner.

# 8 MAKING CHANGES ONE STEP AT A TIME

Once the required architectures, the most important improvements in the architectural process and the practices constituting the architect's role have all been clearly identified, the time has come to implement a professionalization program. A change strategy is defined for this purpose. It establishes the level of ambition, style of the approach to change and the management of expectations. The change strategy is then translated into a concrete action plan.

## 8.1 B-Sure Bank in Action

"OK, it seems to me that everything is now all filled in. We are first going to work on the key areas of alignment with the development process, consultation and then monitoring. As for architectural products, we'll start with an architecture for the customer domain in order to enable Relations Management to gain some insight into customer behavior and sales effectiveness. This is therefore a domain architecture. That all seems quite clear. Let's get the ball rolling." Kevin McAndrew liked the way things were going. There was a clear focus. As far as he could see, there was nothing to stand in the way of a successful process. Or was there?

"Wait a minute," interjected Anne Moreland, "Don't we need to establish something like a strategy or plan of attack first? To my mind, the recent past has taught us at least one lesson – we have to manage expectations! And how do we intend to increase the organization's involvement in our activities? What things are we going to communicate? And how quickly do we actually want to move through the maturity matrix? What are our ambitions?"

## 8.2 Effective Change

Based on the changes that the organization has in store, we can determine the architecture that is required. With the help of the Architecture Maturity Matrix, we can identify those aspects of the architectural process that must be given focus. We can also determine where the strengths of the architecture team lie and where improvements might be made. It is now up to us to translate this knowledge into concrete activities that contribute value to the organization and increase the effectiveness of the architecture function. This is not something that we can do in isolation. There are too many stakeholders involved with the architecture, and the effective employment of architecture affects too many of the organization's processes to permit such seclusion. For the same reason, it is crucial that the manner in which we realize the intended improvements suits the structure, culture and working procedures of the organization and the capacity of the architects. It still remains for us to translate the established focal points into concrete actions that suit our organization, and to manage these actions so as to launch an effective trajectory of change. It is best to establish an overall strategy and approach to accomplish these tasks. This will be our guiding principle in drafting successive action plans.

It is advisable to undertake the intended professionalization in a step-by-step manner. This means that we develop a strategy for a longer term but implement it in a series of planned steps. A Quarterly Plan is an action plan for the upcoming three months. Near the end of the three months, the subsequent Quarterly Plan is then drafted. The quarterly plans provide the necessary dynamism. The overall change strategy safeguards continuity and consistency.

## 8.3 Change Strategy: Ambition, Style and Expectation Management

Architecture cannot be employed without the resulting manner of working and thinking having an enormous impact on the organization. To channel this organizational involvement effectively, it is important to consider the best way of achieving the desired improvement, in advance. This change strategy establishes the parameters for activities to be performed in the quarterly plans. It is concerned with the following factors:

- *Level of ambition governing architectural practice*. How quickly do we want to have architectural practices in place? What will their scope be? When must the first results appear? Where do we want to be in about one year? In short, what is the general time line?

- *Style of change.* How systematically are we going to work? To what extent are we going to keep stakeholders informed about the trajectory of change? Which employees are going to take an active role in the process? To what degree do we want it to be a learning process?

— *Expectation management.* How do we ensure that the appropriate expectations exist in the organization (expectations that we can actually fulfill)?

The level of ambition has an effect on the speed at which we expect to see results. How quickly do we want architectural practices to be fully developed?

The other two factors (style of change and expectation management) involve managing the trajectory of change. What style will we employ? How are we going to manage the view that the organization has of the change process and, consequently, of the architecture function? The answer to this last question determines how we will successfully integrate the architecture function within the organization.

## 8.4 The Organization Sets the Pace

To stay on the chosen course, we divide general ambitions for the maturity of the architecture function into a series of goals with deadlines. This establishes a time frame composed of time boxes for accomplishing the many facets of the architecture function.

First we set the level of ambition by asking what position the architecture is expected to have in the organization, say, two years from now. Then we plot the course to get there. We could decide to work first on the link with Strategic Dialogue (i.e. on the relationship with business) and then focus our sights on the development process – or precisely the other way around. We could also make choices about scope: do we want to immediately set up the architecture function organization-wide, or do we first concentrate on the division where the most development is occurring and the need for architecture is greatest?

The choices that we make here not only depend on our score in the Architecture Maturity Matrix but also on what is possible and feasible given the as-is state. Ambitions must be realistic. They might demand a certain effort, but they must ultimately be achievable. Consider these factors:

— *Organizational culture.* A process-focused culture provides a favorable environment for integrating architecture into the development processes. A results-focused culture generally provides a more productive basis for demonstrating the added value of architecture in the Strategic Dialogue. In a rigid culture, the employees are accustomed to complying with frameworks and norms and will more readily accept architecture as a framework instrument than will employees working in a relaxed culture where they are used to a great deal of freedom.

— *Organizational structure.* One of the pitfalls that often hampers architectural practice is uncertainty about roles and responsibilities. It leads to long discussions about the status of the architecture, what need and need not be complied with, and who actually has the say.

— *Leadership.* By leadership, we mean the extent to which the organization is governed by a consistent and coherent business and IT vision and strategy. Vision and strategy provide a favorable basis and environment for architecture. If there is no shared vision and strategy, this usually indicates that implementing architectural practices may meet with resistance and require extra effort.

— *Process standards.* If an organization is accustomed to using standardized processes like project management and system development, it is easier to align architecture and architects' roles with existing practices than to deal with each project on an individual basis.

— *Knowledge and skills.* It is not surprising that the knowledge and skills possessed by the architects largely affect the speed with which architectural work is accomplished.

If any of these factors hampers the employment of architecture, the level of ambition will have to be lowered. Of course, the organization could decide to do something about such impediments. In that case, it is not just the architecture function that is to be made more effective and professional but the organization as a whole. In practice, we regularly see that the professionalization of architectural practices goes hand in hand with the improvement of IT governance and even the entire IT function.

A financial institution is strongly results-focused. It achieves results through informal mutual agreements about the things to be done and the individuals who will do them. There are no formal consensus processes. The appropriate people for particular jobs are determined following agreements about who should work in specific areas.

The institution is in a transition phase in which it is converting from a monopoly position to a competitive position, which involves a great number of changes in many fields. Management is still adjusting to this change, looking to chart a course. Since IT developments are required for better streamlining, an architecture team is established. This team of architects is assigned to the IT department.

In this environment, the manager of the architecture team has to decide how to go about his work. Given the situation, he decides that a bottom-up approach has the greatest chance of success. There are no formal development processes to hook up with, and management is still exploring too many options to have any clear vision of the future. His strategy is to accept the formal position of architecture for what it is and to concentrate on providing added value immediately. In this way, he wants to demonstrate that architecture makes a contribution to the company. His ambition is, little by little, to gain a foothold for architecture on the basis of its added value.

He searches for any leverage he can use. He sees an opportunity in the multitude of changes confronting the company, and he offers management a steering mechanism with which to direct the content of the changes. It is welcomed with open arms. Individual projects are brought into line by having the architects participate in business cases and high level designs for the projects. In performing these activities, it is the role of the architects to foster as much architectural thinking as possible.

The manager in this example realizes that there is insufficient formal structure to implement the architecture function from top down. For that reason he does not try to gain acceptance for architectural practices as such. Instead, he decides to apply architectural thinking in a more implicit manner, wherever possible. The full potential of architecture cannot be realized in this way, but this is the best that can be achieved in the given situation. If the organization wants to get more out of architecture, it will have to initiate a broader professionalization program.

Insofar as the state of architecture is concerned, the level of ambition is established by means of the 18 key areas from Chapter 6. To establish the level of ambition, the deadlines for the levels in each of the areas need to be placed in the appropriate time sequence.

Table 8.1 provides an example. In this table, the Architecture Maturity Matrix is converted into a time line. In it, the variables Q2 through Q8 stand for the second through eighth quarters of the professionalization trajectory. In this case, the program extends over two years. In the first six months (up to and including the second quarter), work is performed on the levels shown in column Q2. These are the levels corresponding to stages 1 through 3 in the Maturity Matrix. In the next two quarters (six months), an effort is made to attain stage 6. These are the levels indicated in column Q4. The following two quarters involve work on stage 8 and then 10. Finally, the last two quarters are dedicated to attaining stage 13. The basic matrix in Table 8.1 can be used to construct a similar matrix for

### *Table 8.1* Levels distributed over time

| Key area | Q2 | Q4 | Q5 | Q6 | Q8 |
|---|---|---|---|---|---|
| Development of architecture | Architecture undertaken in projects | Architecture as a continuous process | Architecture as a facilitation process | – | – |
| Use of architecture | Architecture used informatively | Architecture used to steer content | – | Architecture integrated into the organization | – |
| Alignment with business | Architecture tested for compatibility with business goals | Architectural process geared to business goals | – | Architectural process is an integral component of business | – |
| Alignment with the development process | Ad hoc | Structural | Interactive | – | – |
| Alignment with operations | – | Ad hoc | Structural | Interactive | – |
| Relationship to the as-is state | – | Attention to the as-is state | Attention to migration | – | – |
| Roles and responsibilities | Responsibility for architectural content assigned | Management responsible for the architectural process | – | Senior management responsible for the effect of architecture | – |
| Coordination of developments | – | Steering the content in each project | – | Coherence among projects | – |
| Monitoring | Reactive monitoring | Proactive monitoring | Embedded monitoring | Integrated monitoring | – |
| Quality management | – | – | Retrospective validation | Quality process developed | Embedded quality policy |
| Maintenance of the architectural process | – | Maintenance performed in a fragmented manner | Maintenance procedures are established | Continuous process improvement | – |
| Maintenance of architectural deliverables | – | Maintenance performed in a fragmented manner | Maintenance procedures are established | – | A maintenance policy exists |
| Commitment and motivation | Allocation of budget and time | Architecture integrated into processes of change | Continuous architectural improvement accepted by organization | – | – |
| Architectural roles and training | Role recognized | Role described | Role supported | – | Role valued |
| Use of an architectural method | Project specific | – | – | Organization generic | Organizationally optimizing R&D activities |
| Consultation | Internal architectural meetings | Meetings with sponsors and users of architecture | All-encompassing discussions about the quality of the architectural processes in the organization | – | – |
| Architectural tools | – | Ad hoc and product based | – | Structural and process based | Integration of tools |
| Budgeting and planning | Project specific | – | – | Organization generic | Optimizing |

each specific situation. The accomplished levels are marked, the time lines made shorter or longer, and the levels shifted as required by the situation. Levels may be shifted, for example, when the work on a specific area is delayed because the organization is not ready for it. Management can also choose not to develop the organization as far as stage 13 – in that case, a number of the higher levels should be removed from the table.

Table 8.1 deals with the process side. It is a tool for determining levels of ambition in the professionalization of architectural practices. It helps us to implement an environment in which we can supply the architectures required by the organization when they are required. Table 8.1 does not show the types of architectures that are needed; that is addressed in our Quarterly Plan. After all, if we architects want to undertake developments where there is actual need, we can hardly do this by planning two years ahead. We have to learn how to deliver an architecture quickly and we must decide, every three months, which architecture to work on over the coming three months.

To facilitate communication, we can visualize the level of ambition by using the Quadrant Model, as illustrated in Figure 8.1. This figure indicates that, in the given scenario, we want to first concentrate on increasing the content quality of the architecture and the relationship with business. Subsequently, we will shift the focus to using architecture in guiding projects. Translated into the DYA Model, the emphasis is first laid on Architectural Services and the Strategic Dialogue and then on Development with(out) Architecture. A choice like this can be suitable where the key areas relating to the level of architectural thinking have been underemphasized up to this point. It might also be motivated by the realization that the greatest opportunities for the organization lie in the realm of Strategic Dialogue.

Throughout the trajectory of change, the level of ambition should be used as a guiding principle to ensure that we are constantly working on the right parts of the process and that we ultimately achieve a professional architecture function. Determining specific activities to perform will be left to the Quarterly Plan.

## 8.5 Participation, Positioning and Pathway to Professionalism

We need to know what we want to achieve, but before we plunge into all types of activities we should also consider how best to achieve the results. In other words, what is the style of change? Do we, as architects, withdraw for six months in order to put our own house in order, or do we engage the organization right from

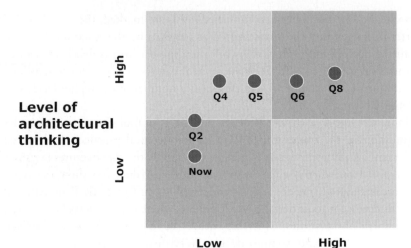

*Figure 8.1* **Level of ambition over time**

the start? And if we involve the organization, how do we go about it? Are we going to organize workshops, make presentations or individually visit each of the most important stakeholders? In general, how actively do we want stakeholders to participate in architecture? Is it necessary to provide an incentive to make employees enthusiastic?

Like the level of ambition, the style of change must also suit the organization. Complying with the dominant standards and values of the organization improves the chances that the initiative will be accepted. The change strategy should address these issues:

— *Participation*: should all the work be performed by a small team (of architects) or should business analysts and designers be contributing ideas and work right from the start?

— *Positioning*: should the architecture be imposed top down by a central steering body with a mandate from the directors, or should the architecture be implemented as a supportive activity that first has to demonstrate its added value for the organization?

— *Pathway*: is the emphasis in the professionalization trajectory placed on well-planned management, on the fact that it is a collective learning process or on the alignment of various stakeholder interests?

In decisions about participation, positioning and pathway, an important role is played by the organizational culture and structure.

**Participation**

Just the architects
or others as well?

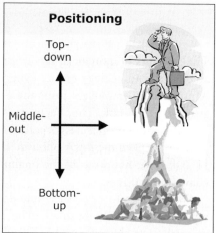

**Positioning**

Top-
down

Middle-
out

Bottom-
up

**Pathway**

Planned          Stakeholders aligned          Learning process

*Figure 8.2* **Participation, positioning and pathway**

In a formal top-down structure with clearly allocated responsibilities, people are more likely to accept and perhaps even expect that the architecture team should assert itself. In an informal culture in which responsibilities are less clear, people will expect more collaboration and may feel that they are being passed over if they have not been involved.

Organization-wide *participation* must be timed carefully. If people are involved too soon, before there is much to show or test, there is a risk of creating the impression that the architecture is all talk and no action. If people are involved too late, they may get the impression that everything has already been decided and their input is irrelevant.

Participation can take many forms. Employees may be directly involved in architectural activities – for example, as subject-area experts when developing architectures. Employees may also be invited to contribute ideas on how best to set up architectural processes. One way to promote participation is by forming an architectural community: an informal network of persons who are ready to function as a sounding board for all types of issues concerning the professionalization of architectural practices.

The directors of a financial service provider have decided that they must have architecture to achieve greater synergy among the company's four divisions. A number of employees from the IT departments in the four divisions are assigned to this task. They begin energetically but soon realize that, without the involvement of the business departments, nothing will be achieved. The problem is that they need the input of business to evaluate the process architecture. The IT task force has done all the preliminary work but the final validation must come from business.

They decide to organize a one-day seminar with a number of important representatives from business. The morning will be dedicated to collective discussion of the relationship between business and IT, and the afternoon devoted to presenting the results in the architectural domain up to this point. The objective of the seminar is to conclude concrete agreements concerning the participation of the business departments in the rest of the process.

No sooner said than done. And the morning is a great success. The team begins by presenting 20 statements about the collaboration between business and IT. The participants react to the statements. This leads to an extremely significant discussion about mutual expectations, the manner in which both parties view the collaboration between them and the points at which everyone would like to see some improvement. The resolution for the morning is, *We need to speak more often with each other in this manner and in similarly structured occasions. Let's hold a similar seminar every quarter.*

In the afternoon, the latest architectural results are presented. The products are shown and explained in detail. The participants are then asked to take some time to evaluate the process architecture. However, by the time the question is posed, the enthusiasm and energy of the group has been exhausted. After the animated discussions of the morning, the complexity of the presented results catches the participants off guard. The jump is too great.

What we see here is that involving the business departments in architectural thinking was, in itself, well done. The interactive session based on the statements stimulated an open discussion about mutual collaboration, which was clearly appreciated by the participants. Initiating dialogue clarified where shared interests lie and cultivated mutual understanding. What followed was too big a step, however; the participants could only nod politely when presented with the complex products. It would have been better to stop after the morning and hold a number of similar sessions collectively before moving on to the process architecture, even if this meant repeating some steps.

The *positioning* of architecture, like participation, has everything to do with the organizational culture and structure, but also with the attitude of senior management towards architecture. A top-down approach to architecture will be easier to realize in a formal organization, where roles and responsibilities are clearly allocated, than in an informal, relaxed organization. If the structures to support architecture are missing, the architects must take a bottom-up approach whereby they seek leverage and opportunities to provide immediate added value. In a formal organization, the development of a project-start architecture can be made mandatory; in a more informal organization, an architect will have to convince a project manager of the benefit in developing a project-start architecture.

Top-down and bottom-up may, in practice, be combined into a middle-out approach. With the blessing of senior management, architectural frameworks are put in place. At the same time, effort is made to become involved in the most important strategic projects at the earliest possible stage and, on the basis of this collaborative and concerted position, to exercise influence.

Still, experience has shown us that in all organizations, formal or informal, architecture can only be successful if the architects are accepted as experts familiar with the ins and outs of the organization.

Two architects are appointed in one of the small business units of a large institution. It is their task to better streamline developments in the IT field. The culture in the business unit they are entering is based on personal authority: people get things done because they know what they are doing, not because they are performing a certain function.

The architects decide on the following tactic: they collect all the information about the projects that have been or are being undertaken. What design and technical choices have been made? What problems have been encountered? And how will they be resolved? Slowly but surely, they assemble a great deal of knowledge, and they increasingly assume the function of an encyclopedia of projects. Projects that run into difficult choices or problems seek out these architects, to ask them whether other projects have ever dealt with anything similar. And the architects are progressively more able to assist projects by referring to previously discovered solutions or by bringing people into contact with each other. Projects consult these architects at increasingly earlier stages in order to exchange thoughts about possible solutions. Very gradually, the architects take on an increasingly prominent steering role, instead of the role of an information supplier. Later when they decide that a number of frameworks and guidelines need to be established, their proposal is completely accepted.

The architects in this example understand very well that, in the dominant culture, there is no chance of success if they try to establish top-down frameworks in their formal capacity as architects. They will not be accepted and projects will just continue along their own paths. But neither will anyone blow the whistle on this non-compliance. The only way for them to have their architecture accepted is by gaining personal credibility and providing added value. Although such a route is long, it is by far the most effective in the given circumstances.

The third component of the style of change, the *pathway*, has a lot to do with cultural and structural aspects as well as the expectations surrounding the professionalization trajectory. If professionalization is viewed as a learning process for the entire organization, the implication is that not everything is entirely foreseeable: sometimes things have to be tried out, and they do not always go as planned. A great deal of disappointment can be prevented by establishing this from the start.

Time boxing is a helpful concept in designing the pathway. Dividing an overall time frame into a series of small boxes can, for example, prevent too many details from being finalized too much in advance. Often these details turn out not to be functional in practice. It is more effective to form an overall picture of what a project-start architecture must provide and start making them, than to spend weeks of trying to define the ultimate template for a project-start architecture. After three project-start architectures have been made, the right template emerges of its own. The same holds true for describing the overall architectural processes.

Consider providing guidance along the pathway by drafting an architecture handbook, a manual that gradually, over the course of the professionalization process, becomes filled with useful tips, working procedures and explanations for the architect and anyone else working with architecture. The handbook should be to the point, practical and immediately usable. Keeping these criteria in mind and ensuring that the handbook conforms to them reduces the danger of expending a great deal of energy on meta-issues that are not actually relevant.

A pension company decides that the time has come to introduce architecture. The intent is to realize the business goals in a more structured and consistent manner, with less deflection. The company, which considers reliability to be of paramount importance, has a rigid, process-focused culture with strong central management. Processes are precisely described, well documented and implemented strictly according to plan.

Accordingly, the introduction of architectural practices is carried out in a well-planned manner. A project for the "Implementation of Architecture" is set up. The project describes the architectural processes, drafts an initial version of architectural guidelines, defines the role of architecture in system development and the pre-project phase, and identifies the roles and responsibilities. The project team, which includes representatives from all the departments involved on both the business and IT sides, first composes a detailed Project Plan, including a time frame with staggered time boxes. The project goal is defined as, "the company is ready to work with architecture." The final date for the project coincides with the start date on which the company officially and formally begins to employ architectural practices.

Although the project is far from problem-free (due to the fact that time-boxing is used in an organization accustomed to aiming for full completion), this planned approach is clearly the only route to take in this company. Expectation management certainly proves very important in this trajectory too. In particular, expectations about the degree of detail and perfection with which preparatory activities have to be completed (due to the mentioned time-boxing) need to be curtailed. Nevertheless, the company has made a strong start down the architecture path.

Clearly, there is no simple recipe that works for all organizations. The choices made must suit a given organization's specific culture and structure. There will always be trade-offs between what we want to achieve and what is actually achievable.

A very useful trick to employ when developing a change strategy is to examine the change processes or projects in the recent past. Determine which ones were successful and which not. Investigate the telling differences between them. The result, in many cases, is a good guide to a large number of the factors involved in participation, positioning and pathway.

As an aid for arranging architectural practices so that they accord with an organization's manner of thinking and acting, consider De Caluwé and Vermaak's color model. For a detailed explanation of this model, see Appendix 2.

## 8.6  *Expectation Management*

Often, expectations concerning architecture are high. Or on the other hand there may be a great deal of skepticism and a feeling that nothing is going to come of it all, again. No doubt, a lot is promised: costs will decrease, time-to-market become shorter, redundancy be eliminated and immediate answers be given to all complicated questions. And if a legacy problem is involved, it will also be entirely resolved. Let's get going! In short, it is quite easy to heavily disappoint the organization and confirm its skepticism. It is therefore extremely important to be constantly vigilant that management and employees have realistic expectations. Expectation management requires continuous attention and ongoing communication.

As an initial step in expectation management, identify the individuals involved in the architecture: the stakeholders. Who are all the people implicated in architectural practices and what form does their involvement take? How are they affected? What are their interests? It is also important to note the interrelationships among stakeholders: whose opinion holds sway?

In characterizing the stakeholders, distinguish between groups and individuals. Examples of group stakeholders are business strategists, policy makers, process owners, line managers, information managers, program and project managers, information analysts, developers and administrators. In fact, any group is a stakeholder if it performs any of the following functions:

— provides input for the architecture,

— works within the scope of the architecture,

— uses architecture as a control instrument,

— makes decisions concerning architecture.

It is worthwhile to briefly profile each stakeholder group. What is its position in the organization? What are its most prominent interests? What relationship to architecture does it wish to have?

In addition to groups, there are also individual stakeholders. They are people who are conspicuous in the organization because they have authority within their own groups – people who occupy positions of power and whose voices are heard – in short, the trendsetters of the organization.

Once the stakeholders have been catalogued, the next step is to establish how to involve them in the professionalization process. This can vary widely for each stakeholder and depends on his or her profile. The intensity of their involvement

### *Table 8.2* **Communication Matrix**

| Who | Why | About what | When | In what way | By whom |
|-----|-----|-----------|------|-------------|---------|
| The stakeholder group or individual | What do we want to achieve? Inform, consult, collaborate, decide ... | What do we want to communicate about? Process, proposals, achieved results, choices to be made ... | At which time(s) do we want to communicate? Once, periodically, when certain results are achieved ... | In which way do we want to communicate? Presentation, workshop, newsletter, bilateral discussion, interview, email, work review ... | Who undertakes the communication? Manager of architecture, architect, director ... |

depends on what we want to achieve insofar as the stakeholders are concerned. We can record this in a Communication Matrix. It indicates who, in what way, for what end, at what time, with whom and about what a communication occurs. Each line of the matrix represents a communication act.

First of all, a global matrix is constructed. In formulating a Quarterly Plan, a detailed matrix is established for the specific stage. This is also the moment to conduct the Stakeholder Inventory.

The importance of conducting a Stakeholder Inventory and formulating a Communication Matrix cannot be emphasized enough. Communication is an essential factor in the acceptance of architecture. Good communication requires time, and time is generally scarce, but failing to pay sufficient attention to this element is a frequent pitfall. A related pitfall occurs when communication is enthusiastically undertaken in the beginning but any follow-up is forgotten. Initial presentations are given throughout the organization, and these, deliberately or not, arouse expectations. Then everything goes quiet because the team is busy with the development process and forgets to maintain an appropriate level of communication. Constructing a Communication Matrix in advance, and subsequently using it, can avoid this danger.

A pension company has been busy with architecture for some time, but feels that more can be achieved. The architectural content is in good order, but there is no integration of architectural thinking throughout the planning and execution of projects. To address this issue, the company is now seeking to professionalize its architecture. A Communication Matrix is set up to communicate with the more important stakeholders.

### Table 8.3 Sample Communication Matrix

| Who | Why | About what | When | In what way | By whom |
|---|---|---|---|---|---|
| MT IT | Commitment to vision<br><br>Behavior in conformance with process agreements<br><br>Knowledge of implementation status | Vision<br><br>Changes in work procedures | Monthly in MT IT | Presentation, asking for feedback | Manager of Architecture |
| Process / service owner | Commitment to vision<br><br>Behavior in conformance with process agreements | Vision<br><br>Changes in work procedures | Consequences for process / service | Face-to-face with process owner | Someone from DYA project |
| Webportal steering committee | Make agreements about the use of architecture for the webportal | Added value of architecture for webportal | Once with steering committee for the webportal | In a meeting with the steering committee, ask for commitment and make agreements | Manager of Architecture |
| Information managers | Commitment to vision<br><br>Behavior in conformance with process agreements<br><br>Active input | Vision<br><br>Work procedures changed or to be changed<br><br>Required input | Arrange for separate session | Workshop | Senior architect |

## 8.7 The Quarterly Plan

Once the strategy is clear, it is time to turn to drafting the first Quarterly Plan. What activities are we going to undertake in the coming three months? What will be the result?

An entire array of ingredients have now been assembled to assist in drafting a Quarterly Plan:

— A decision needs to be made about what architectural artifacts to produce. The answer will depend on the business goals and the changes required to achieve them.

— The Maturity Matrix provides the basis for determining which processes to address in what order.

— Depending on the architects' level of experience, a form of training or coaching may be desirable.

— The level of ambition we are aiming at as part of our strategy will help us to decide the number of factors that we can handle at one time, as well as the ones that we are better off leaving for later.

— The chosen style determines the manner in which we shall deal with the organization's participation, the formal positioning within the organization and the nature of the pathway we wish to follow.

— The Stakeholder Inventory and Communication Matrix are used to identify how best to maintain communications during the development stage in order to channel and manage the expectations of the organization.

It still remains for us to convert these ingredients into a concrete Quarterly Plan for the upcoming three months. First, two questions need to be answered:

— What is the concrete added value that we want to provide to the organization in the forthcoming developmental stage?

— Is there any leverage that we can use to achieve our goals?

In order not to lose the organization along the way, it is a good idea to focus on the added value that the architecture function delivers. The added value ultimately lies in the goal of working with architecture, but fully achieving this goal can be a long way off – sometimes too far off to exclusively base the added value on it. There is not always time to spend six months settling in and getting ready before having to show any results.

The added value of architecture is not found in the production of architectural documents. Its value needs to come from the effects of these documents and the impact of the architectural thinking underlying them. Such effects can be found in various areas: in clarifying the consequences of choices, in creating more flexible information flows to keep pace with changes in the business, in reducing costs and, of course, in making the organization achieve its business goals. The added value is therefore locatable in the application of architecture, in the manner in which it helps to achieve the organization's goals.

The best way of determining the added value architecture is to speak with the consumers of this value: the stakeholders. For this purpose, we can refer to the Stakeholder Inventory that we compiled as part of our expectation management process. Determining stakeholder needs can be done quite simply and effectively just by talking to them.

*Next port of projects*

We do not have to look too far to find added value: a very simple survey of all the current projects can, in itself, be of great value to management; an agreement that finally puts an end to an ongoing discussion can suddenly move a project further along.

As the last component of the Quarterly Plan, leverage consists of developments in the organization where architecture can directly complement and enhance the progress being made, thereby increasing architecture's prominence and the organizational buy-in. If the accounting department is, for example, implementing portfolio management, we can link up with it in order to introduce portfolio content management instead of developing a separate initiative. Once we have some notion of the available opportunities for leverage, as well as the areas in which added value can be provided in the short term, we can then complete our Quarterly Plan.

1. We list the possible activities in the following manner:

   - The Maturity Matrix reveals the key areas on which to focus. These are translated into concrete actions that comply with (1) the set level of ambition, (2) the style we have chosen for participation, positioning and pathway, (3) the knowledge and experience of the architects, and (4) any leverage that we have identified.

   - Based on the current business goals of the organization and the changes that are in store, we define the architecture on which we are going to work in the coming three months.

   - Opportunities that offer added value over the short term are then converted into concrete activities.

   - Using the Communication Matrix, we identify the desired communication activities.

2. Given our available capacity, we select from the list of activities the ones that we are actually going to undertake in the next three months. In so doing, we ensure that there is a good balance between professionalization, the offering of added value and communication.

3. We allocate the available capacity to the activities. It is advisable to assign architects as much as possible to work in (interchanging) pairs, a practice that promotes quality and the sharing of knowledge among architects.

On the basis of the Maturity Matrix, a financial institution decides that work in the coming period will focus on two concerns:

— strengthening the relationship with business,

— anchoring architectural thought in the new development process that is currently being implemented.

To deal with the first issue, the vision, added value and role of architecture must be clarified and used to start dialogue with the information managers and business units. To address the second issue, a link must be forged with the existing "IT processes" project, which is working on the improvement of the system development processes.

The work on the first issue lays the foundation and is directed at gaining support for architecture. By means of interactive sessions and a joint assessment based on the Maturity Matrix, a collective conception of the use and role of architecture can be established. Work in the second area is more practical and technical, involving participation in the formal description of the processes and the planned implementation of newly described practices.

| Activity | Phase 1 | | | | Phase 2 |
|---|---|---|---|---|---|
| | 30/4 | 31/5 | 15/6 | 31/7 | |
| Vision document | ▓ | | | | |
| Services catalogue A&A | ▓ | | | | |
| Communication plan | | ▓ | | | |
| Communication | | | ▓ | ▓ | ▓ |
| First alignment with IM | | ▓ | | | |
| Architecture assessment IM | | | | | |
| Second alignment with IM | | | ▓ | | |
| Formal agreements strat. collab. | | | | ▓ | |
| Execution plan per business unit | | | | ▓ | |
| Embedding intake & proposal | In IT processes | | | | |
| Embedding preparation | | | In IT processes | | |

*Figure 8.3* **Sample Quarterly Plan**

Once the three months are over, we will then evaluate the results and draft a new Quarterly Plan for the following three months.

## *8.8  B-Sure Bank's Strategy and Quarterly Plan*

B-Sure Bank has decided to professionalize its architectural practices by making them more formalized, integrated and effective. First of all, a strategy is formulated, then quarterly plans are developed based on that strategy. The initial step in the strategy is to determine the level of ambition. Arnold Hedges examines the key factors and comes up with the following analysis.

B-Sure Bank is more results-focused than process-focused. Employees are dealt with in terms of what they achieve rather than their adherence to processes. A very relaxed culture is predominant, and people are evaluated on their merits more than on their function. This does not mean that anarchy reigns. Management certainly has things firmly in hand, and decisions by bodies such as the architecture board are taken very seriously. The manner in which decisions originate is, however, not always clear to an outsider.

The leadership at B-Sure Bank is solid. Senior management has a clear vision of the future. The purposes for employing architecture are also clear. It is meant to identify the opportunities for synergy resulting from the recent merger and to take advantage of them.

On paper, incorporating architecture into the organization's work procedures is not so difficult. These have already been described. Architectural aspects can simply be added to this document. But Arnold recognizes a problem: in practice, the document is not used by the organization and projects are just left to go their own way.

The architects are sufficiently well trained and knowledgeable. Communication skills are also sufficiently well developed. It must be said, however, that the team displays a tendency to think from inside out. The architects are more preoccupied with perfecting artifacts than responding to the needs of the organization. Customer focus could be improved.

Arnold concludes that the climate is favorable enough to initiate the next step in architectural thinking. The biggest difficulty will likely be the lack of discipline, complicated by the absence of processes to enforce this discipline. These shortcomings will hamper full compliance with plans and agreements. Still, given the recent comments by Peter Wilder about not seeing any progress, it is necessary that a number of substantial improvements should be implemented within a year. After that he can work on optimization.

To improve the process component of architecture, Arnold composes a one-year Ambition Matrix. He plots the levels already attained in the first column. For the first quarter, his decision is to focus purely on the areas that will promote the integration of architecture within the organization. He will then deal with the

## *Table 8.4* B-Sure Bank's Ambition Matrix

| Key area | Present | Q1 | Q3 | Q5 |
|---|---|---|---|---|
| Development of architecture | Architecture undertaken in projects | – | Architecture as a continuous process | Architecture as a facilitation process |
| Use of architecture | Architecture used informatively | Architecture used to steer content | – | Architecture integrated into the organization |
| Alignment with business | Architecture tested against the business goals / architectural process geared to business goals | – | – | – |
| Alignment with the development process | – | Ad hoc | Structural | Interactive |
| Alignment with operations | – | Ad hoc | – | Structural |
| Relationship to the as-is state | – | Attention to the as-is state | – | Attention to migration |
| Roles and responsibilities | Responsibility for architectural content assigned | Management responsible for the architectural process | – | – |
| Coordination of developments | – | – | Steering the content in each project | Coherence among projects |
| Monitoring | – | Reactive monitoring | Proactive monitoring | Embedded monitoring |
| Quality management | – | – | Retrospective validation | Quality process developed |
| Maintenance of the architectural process | – | – | Maintenance performed in a fragmented manner | Maintenance procedures are established |
| Maintenance of architectural deliverables | Maintenance performed in a fragmented manner | – | Maintenance procedures are established | – |
| Commitment and motivation | Allocation of budget and time | – | Architecture integrated into processes of change | – |
| Architectural roles and training | Role recognized | – | Role described | Role supported |
| Use of an architectural method | Project specific | – | – | Organization generic |
| Consultation | – | Internal architectural meetings | Meetings with sponsors and users of architecture | All-encompassing discussions about the quality of the architectural processes in the organization |
| Architectural tools | Ad hoc and product based | – | – | Structural and process based |
| Budgeting and planning | Project specific | – | – | Organization generic |

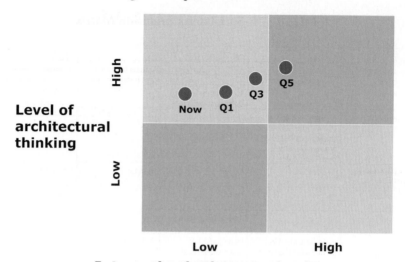

*Figure 8.4* **B-Sure Bank's ambition pathway**

level of architectural thinking in order to prevent it from being neglected. He also decides that, in his planning, he will not look beyond stages 9–10 in the Maturity Matrix.

To facilitate communication, Arnold maps the Ambition Matrix onto the Quadrant Model (Figure 8.4). It shows that the architects want to make a move to the right and then slightly upward.

The next step is to develop a change strategy in which the participation, positioning and pathway are specified. What *participation* should be is instantly clear to Arnold. Given the fact that the architects are actually operating somewhat in isolation, it seems crucial that the rest of the organization become involved in the improvement process. Otherwise, the isolation will never be broken down. He proposes to engage sponsors by having his teams consult with their contact persons about the ways in which architecture might play a key role in project decision making and, of course, the reasons why this is important. And project managers could be actively involved in the introduction of project-start architecture. If he can demonstrate to them that there is something useful here, and help them to appreciate the benefits in a concrete way, that will be a big step.

Insofar as the *positioning* of architecture is concerned, nothing more needs to be done. Architecture already has an official status. But it would be ineffective to take a formal stand. It would be more effective to strengthen the conviction of

## *Table 8.5* B-Sure Bank Stakeholder Inventory

| Stakeholder | Interests |
| --- | --- |
| Board of directors | Wants system updates to be quicker and less expensive, but this is difficult with the organization's old and complex systems. <br> Management must be made more accountable for achieving deadlines and targets. Because processes and systems are so intertwined, no one takes responsibility. This must be broken down. <br> Synergy will result in substantial savings (in the tens of millions). It doesn't matter if the organization is turned inside out to accomplish this. |
| Architecture board | Has the assignment of actually realizing the synergy opportunities resulting from the merger. Sees architecture as the most important instrument for this purpose. |
| Director of Banking (formerly with B-Bank) | Feels that B-Bank had everything well in hand – in any case, better than Personality. |
| Director of Investment (formerly with Virtuality) | Is convinced that Virtuality leads the field insofar as the internet and new technologies are concerned. In his eyes, such developments are extremely important to Investment. <br> He is hesitant about architecture because Investment is a whole different ball game than banking and insurance are, and must not be developed using the same playing rules. <br> He sees the costs of management and of maintenance and operations going up, but perhaps that is just the price you have to pay to keep up with the times. |
| Director of Insurance (formerly with Personality) | Sees his division as the largest, therefore the most important. Believes Personality's customers were completely satisfied and that Personality was better than Virtuality, where they took a lot of risks. <br> He feels that operations are becoming very large and complex and that he must be careful not to lose control. <br> He regards architecture as a tool with which he can better manage his division, but he is extremely impatient. Complains that he sees too few results from the architects. |
| Information Manager for Banking | Feels that he has his affairs in order. Sees little added value in architecture but does not object to it. |
| Information Manager for Investment | Is a big supporter of using standard packages. Strikes him that it is rather difficult to keep on top of the multitude of packages and technologies. Is receptive to suggestions about how they can be better streamlined. |
| Information Manager for Insurance | Is fairly conservative: as long as customers are happy, believes he's obviously doing the right thing. He is not at all comfortable with the internet, but he recognizes that it brings the whole world to his door, so he's on the verge of drafting a policy plan and has already inquired if architecture can help. His view of architecture seems to be that even if it doesn't help, it doesn't hurt either. |
| Department managers in Banking | Generally feel that everything is going well in their division. Priority for improvements must be given to Insurance, where things are in a real mess and potential synergy gains are obvious everywhere. |
| Department managers in Investment | See Investment as a completely independent business within B-Sure Bank. Synergy is fine, as long as you leave Investment alone. |
| Department Managers in Insurance | Are very busy keeping their own house in order. There are quite a few operational problems, which were not improved by the shake-up. Something has to be done. But everyone is so busy putting out bush fires that it's difficult to give any thought to structural matters. |
| IT Manager | His most prominent concern is improving service to the company. If architecture can help with that, all the better. |
| Project managers | Have noticed that it is not easy to successfully complete a project. The requirements are never stable and the deadlines are always much too short. Business does not understand why simple adjustments take so much time. Projects are becoming increasingly larger. Whenever something needs to be adjusted, it seems like everything is related to everything else. |
| Operations | Is involved with a large variety of software and hardware, all of which needs to be managed. Is frequently caught off guard by new technology. Is extremely favorable to architecture because it is regarded as a means of controlling the barrage of new developments. |
| Relations Management | Has little interest in architecture. In fact, considers anything related to processes and IT to be tiresome, and does not want to get involved. |

his colleagues in the organization that architecture adds value; Arnold chooses to present himself as a service provider rather than a controller.

The *pathway* merits some thought. Arnold will primarily concentrate on bringing the various stakeholders onside in relation to B-Sure Bank's information systems. If that is successful, he will have demonstrated the use of architecture. The pathway will involve a lot of conversation.

Since interaction and feedback is so important, a Communication Matrix is no superfluous luxury. Arnold first catalogues the stakeholders (Table 8.5). Although the organization has gone through a shake-up, Arnold notices that the old bloodlines are still dominant.

Using the Stakeholder Inventory, Arnold produces a Communication Matrix (Table 8.6). It shows when, why and how information about the architecture professionalization trajectory will be presented to the various stakeholders.

Arnold has now assembled all the ingredients he needs to generate the first Quarterly Plan for the coming three months. He has covered everything, and plans activities where action is needed:

*Activities based on the Maturity Matrix and the Ambition Matrix derived from it (the focus of Q1):*

1. Introduce project-start architecture (use of architecture).

2. Promote greater understanding for architecture among project managers and operational administrators (alignment with development processes, alignment with operations).

3. Formulate policy for dealing with the installed base, which is to say the existing processes, systems and infrastructure (relationship to the as-is state).

4. Have a process owner appointed for the architectural process (roles and responsibilities).

5. Have the steering groups take verifying compliance with architecture more seriously (monitoring).

6. Focus architecture meetings more on content (consultation).

*Action aimed at developing architectures that reflect the business goals of B-Sure Bank:*

7. Develop a domain architecture for the customer domain.

### *Table 8.6* B-Sure Bank Communication Matrix

| Who | Why | About what | When | In what way | By whom |
|---|---|---|---|---|---|
| Architecture board | To make it harder to deviate from architecture | Consequences of deviating from architecture; how to deal with any unavoidable deviations | Week 6; in preparation for this, hold advanced bilateral discussions with directors | Set aside 45 minutes in quarterly meeting for presentation and discussion | Arnold |
| Department managers in divisions | To include architecture in project assignments | Consequences of deviating from architecture; how to deviate less; how to deal with unavoidable deviations | Week 10-11; in preceding weeks, coordinate with information managers | Bilateral discussions | Customer teams together with information managers |
| Paul Chambers, Project Manager | To collaborate on project-start architecture (PSA); run a pilot together | What is PSA? Why PSA? How to design a PSA? | Week 2-3 | Bilateral discussion | Anne |
| Karen Poole, Project Manager | To collaborate on PSA; run a pilot together | What is PSA? Why PSA? How can PSA be designed? | Week 2-3 | Bilateral discussion | Anne |
| Information managers; IT Manager | To collectively formulate a vision regarding information flows | Requirements of information flows; IT possibilities | Week 9 | Workshop | Arnold, Kevin |
| Project managers | To define architecture's role in projects | Why architecture? What does architecture mean for projects? | Week 1 | Set aside a half hour in project-manager meeting for presentation and discussion | Anne |
| Operations | To define architecture's role insofar as maintenance is concerned | Why architecture? What does architecture mean for maintenance? | Week 2 | Set aside a half hour in operations departmental meeting for presentation and discussion | Anne |
| Entire organization | To provide information about the trajectory | Purpose and progress of trajectory | First Monday of the month | Newsletter | Fred |

*Action on training architects*:

8. Start intervision.

*Action to bring added value in the short term*:

9. Provide the architecture board with insight about the coherence of current projects.

*Communication activities:*

10. Make presentation to architecture board.

11. Make presentation at project manager meeting (part of #2).

12. Make presentation at operations department meeting (part of #2).

13. Hold discussions with divisional department managers together with information managers (part of #5).

14. Organize workshop for information managers and head of IT.

15. Involve Paul Chambers or Karen Poole in project-start architecture pilot (part of #1).

16. Set up newsletter.

Not counting the communication activities that are part of other activities, Arnold is left with 12 separate activities for the coming quarter. He has 15 architects available to him, and he does not anticipate having to scrap anything on this list. It should be possible to accomplish everything. If capacity problems should arise, activity 3 (formulating policy to deal with the installed base) could be delayed until the next quarter.

Arnold immediately sets up a meeting with his architects in order to take them through the Quarterly Plan and to attach names to actions. After checking with Peter Wilder, Arnold is able to come up with a final plan.

---

**Architecture Quarterly Plan**

**Background**

This Quarterly Plan outlines the activities of the architecture department in the first quarter of next year (Q1). The goal of Q1 is better integration of architecture throughout the organization. The activities included in this plan are strongly based on a SWOT analysis of the architectural practices at B-Sure Bank, followed by further analysis of the organizational needs and opportunities relating to architecture. The plan represents the first phase of an improvement process that will take all of the coming year and ultimately aims to streamline processes and deploy IT more effectively at B-Sure Bank.

**Results**

Phase 1 of the improvement trajectory, which this plan describes, will produce the following results at B-Sure Bank within a period of three months:

1. A domain architecture has been drafted for the customer domain as specified in the Customer Domain Project Plan.

2. An overview has been conducted of the coherence between existing and planned projects.

3. There are policies on how to deal with the currently installed base.

4. Project-start architecture has been introduced as an instrument and applied in at least one pilot project.

5. Architecture is better integrated into the change processes at B-Sure Bank (the architectural process has one process owner; steering committees are better able to monitor architectural practices in projects and there is more understanding among project managers and operational administrators for architecture).

6. There is better communication about architectural practices among architects as well as between architects and other stakeholders (timely communication is monitored on the basis of a concrete communication plan, a biweekly architectural meeting for all architects and a monthly newsletter for the whole organization).

### Planning

The table below lists the activities that will be performed in order to achieve the stated results, the estimated hours required for each activity and the person(s) charged with the task.

*Table 8.7* **Estimated activities for B-Sure Bank architecture Quarterly Plan**

| No. | Activity | Required hours | Assigned personnel |
|-----|----------|----------------|--------------------|
| 1 | Develop a domain architecture for the customer domain | 560 | Mary, Peter, Hank |
| 2 | Survey of current projects | 240 | Anne, Mary, Helen |
| 3 | Formulate policy on installed base | 200 | John, Bill |
| 4 | Introduce project-start architecture | | |

| No. | Activity | Required hours | Assigned personnel |
|-----|----------|----------------|--------------------|
| 4.1 | Agreement with project managers | 24 | Anne, Hank |
| 4.2 | Conduct pilot | 76 | Anne, Hank |
| 5 | Process owner architectural process | 16 | Arnold |
| 6 | Better control by steering committees | 80 | Kevin, account teams |
| 7 | Dialogue with project and operations | 80 | Anne, Kevin |
| 8 | Architecture meetings | | |
| 8.1 | Organizing architecture meetings | 16 | Kevin, Bill |
| 8.2 | Participation in architecture meetings | 150 | All |
| 9 | Intervision | | |
| 9.1 | Start intervision | 24 | Anne |
| 9.2 | Implement intervision | 100 | Fred, Anne, John, Kevin, Mary |
| 10 | Architecture board presentation | 20 | Arnold |
| 11 | Workshop for information managers and head of IT | 40 | Arnold, Kevin |
| 12 | Setting up newsletter | 32 | Fred, Mary |
| 13 | Project management, control and evaluation | 16 | Arnold |
| | Total time required | 1674 | |

With a total of 15 architects, this means that the architects must spend an average of 8 hours per week on the improvement process. Since not all architects are involved in the plan to the same extent, the commitment will amount to 1 to 2 hours a week for some and about 16 hours for others. All architects will attend the architect meeting. Intervision is open to all architects, but participation is on a voluntary basis. The time not spent on the improvement process will be employed in supporting projects and in exploring unexpected opportunities that undoubtedly will crop up.

The program commences in week 1 (January 1) and terminates in week 14 (March 31). The total duration is 14 weeks. The lightly shaded cells indicate that an activity will be worked on during the specific week. The darkly shaded cells indicate milestones, explained further after the diagram.

***Table 8.8*** **Schedule of activities for B-Sure Bank architecture Quarterly Plan**

| N° | Activity | 1 | 2 | 3 | 4 | 5 | 6 | 7 | 8 | 9 | 10 | 11 | 12 | 13 | 14 |
|----|----------|---|---|---|---|---|---|---|---|---|----|----|----|----|----|
| 1 | Domain arch. customer domain | | | | | | | | | | | ■ | | | |
| 2 | Survey current projects | | | | | | ■ | | | | | | | | |
| 3 | Formulate policy on installed base | | | | | | | | | | | | | | ■ |
| 4 | Project-start architecture | | | | | | | | | | | | | | |
| 4.1 | Agreement project managers | | ■ | | | | | | | | | | | | |
| 4.2 | Conduct pilot | | | | | | | | | | | ■ | | | |
| 5 | Process owner architectural process | | | | | | | | ■ | | | | | | |
| 6 | Control by steering committees | | | | | | | ■ | | | | | | | |
| 7 | Dialogue project/operations | | | ■ | | | | | | | ■ | | | | |
| 8 | Architecture meetings | | | | | | | | | | | | | | |
| 8.1 | Organizing architecture meetings | | | | | | | | | | | | | | |
| 8.2 | Participation in architecture meetings | | | | | | | | | | | | | | |
| 9 | Intervision | | | | | | | | | | | | | | |
| 9.1 | Start intervision | | | | | | | | | ■ | | | | | |
| 9.2 | Implement intervision | | | | | | | | | | | | | | |
| 10 | Architecture board presentation | | | | | | ■ | | | | | | | | |
| 11 | Information/IT management workshop | | | | | | | | ■ | | | | | | |
| 12 | Set up newsletter | | | | | ■ | | | | ■ | | | | | |
| 13 | Project management | | | | | | | | | | | | | | |

A number of activities, such as the architecture meetings, intervision and project management, either recur or are continuous. No specific milestones are set for them.

The following milestones are identifiable:

***Table 8.9*** **Schedule of milestones for B-Sure Bank architecture Quarterly Plan**

| Week | Milestone | Activity |
|------|-----------|----------|
| 3 | An initial presentation given to project managers and operations | 7 |
| 5 | First newsletter distributed | 12 |
| 6 | Survey of current and planned projects ready | 2 |
| 6 | Presentation made to architecture board | 10 |

| Week | Milestone | Activity |
|------|-----------|----------|
| 7 | Interviews with information managers held | 6 |
| 8 | Process owner of architectural process identified | 5 |
| 9 | First intervision meeting | 9.1 |
| 9 | Workshop for information managers and IT manager | 11 |
| 10 | Second presentation to project managers and operations | 7 |
| 10 | Second newsletter distributed | 12 |
| 11 | Domain architecture for customer domain ready | 1 |
| 12 | First project-start architecture pilot ready | 4.2 |
| 12 | Discussions with divisional department heads held | 6 |
| 14 | Policy on installed base formulated | 3 |

# 9 CONCLUSION

## 9.1 Architecture Works

Architecture has to work. It must make noticeable contributions to achieving business goals. To accomplish this, it must be professional and versatile. A professional architecture function is one that can balance content and process, that can effectively answer the following questions:

— What do we want to achieve by adopting architecture?

— What architectures do we require?

— How and with which people do we develop the architectures?

— How do we succeed at permanently embedding architectural thinking and practices in the organization?

— How are we going to train our architects?

In this book, you find tips and instruments to help answer these questions. Additionally, you can read how to piece together a professionalization trajectory to increase the effectiveness of architectural practices, one step at a time. You can create a trajectory that devotes equal amounts of attention to the rapid provision of added value and the conception and maturation of the architectural process.

Here are the key messages that we wanted to get across with this book:

— Pay sufficient attention to the value added by architectural practices to your organization. Ensure that the objectives that you want to achieve with architecture are sufficiently clear to everyone, including the architects. Maintaining a clear vision keeps you on course and is an indispensable guiding principle when setting priorities and making choices. It prevents your architects from getting lost in models where the goals become increasingly vague.

— Develop the architectures that are required to accomplish the business goal: no more and no less. Architecture must be accountable to business needs, and must steer the content of the changes occurring in your organization so that they fit in with the whole. Make sure that you have useful architectures for accomplishing this. Also be attentive to the nature of the intended architecture: are you dealing with an enterprise architecture, a domain architecture or a project-start architecture?

— Working with architecture is multifaceted. It is impossible to take on everything at once – if you tried, you wouldn't be able to provide any added value. Therefore, you must set priorities in professionalizing the architecture function. The Architecture Maturity Matrix with associated suggestions for improvement provides assistance in this regard.

— Content and process are important, but the make-up of the architect is also a crucial success factor. The degree of customer focus, willingness to collaborate and share knowledge, expertise and ability to see another point of view are extremely important qualities for an architect. Consequently, pay attention to coaching and mentoring in developing your architects.

— Architecture is not just something for architects. Architecture controls the organization's trajectory of change, and the more professional and effective the architectural practices, the better for the entire organization. Architectural practices require careful planning and widespread support. Formulate a change strategy with a realistic ambition and attention to positioning, participation and pathway. Actively engage in expectation management.

This book has provided you with a number of tools for developing architectural practices:

— The vision document keeps you on course and helps you to clearly demonstrate the added value of architecture.

— The Project Plan established prior to developing an architecture ensures that you give advance consideration to such important issues as purpose, target group, perspective, usability and effectiveness of the architecture.

— The architectural framework helps to manage multiple interrelated architectures.

— The Quadrant Model can be used to perform a SWOT analysis to weigh the balance between thought and action.

— The DYA Model is a handy instrument to investigate the processes underlying architectural practices in detail. It helps to cultivate a growing awareness among managers, architects and operators about their own working procedures.

— With the Architecture Maturity Matrix, you can establish where you are insofar as architectural processes are concerned and where you must target your improvements. It also identifies concrete steps for improvement.

— The Communication Matrix enables you to determine how you will involve the stakeholders of architecture in the architectural practices and how you can respond to their expectations.

— Finally, the Quarterly Plan helps you to plan improvements over a three-month period and see recognizable results.

Many things are involved in successful architectural practices. The development of a good architecture is only the beginning. Working with architecture affects the entire organization. Therefore, the introduction of architectural practices initiates a trajectory of change. The changes, if well targeted, can have a large impact on the effectiveness of the organization. Using the instruments, tips and approach of this book, you can successfully manage the trajectory of change and enable architecture to truly work for your organization. Ultimately, initiating effective architectural practices gives your organization the power to respond quickly to changes generally.

## 9.2  B-Sure Bank at Full Burn

B-Sure Bank has now been working with architecture for about one and a half years. One of the most important contributions architecture has made is that a great deal of redundancy in processes and systems has been eliminated. The organization as a whole has become much more agile.

Arnold Hedges, the manager of the architecture department, considers it no longer necessary to have a large group of architects at the central level. A small group of enterprise architects will suffice. However in the various business units and the IT division further development is desirable, so there is a need to assign information architects to the Banking, Insurance and Investment divisions and IT architects to the IT division. In a proposal to the directors, Arnold describes the new architecture distribution and defines the roles of the enterprise, information and IT architects.

To the board of directors

In the past year and a half, we have spent a great deal of energy in establishing architectural practices at B-Sure Bank. This has not occurred without a struggle, but we have certainly made a substantial contribution to the transformation of the bank into a "lean & mean" organization able to quickly respond to signals from the market. The time has now come to review the position of the architecture function at B-Sure Bank.

Whereas we have, in the last while, been primarily concerned with purging redundant functions, processes and systems from all sectors of B-Sure Bank, it is now important to assist the various divisions in converting business initiatives as quickly as possible into effective solutions. This must be done in coordination with all the other changes that are occurring.

In this respect, I propose that the business/information architects be assigned to the business divisions and the IT architects to the IT division. At the central level, it will be sufficient to have three enterprise architects. They will monitor developments in the divisions, keep them in step with each other and ensure that architectures are developed in a consistent manner. I propose that each business division be allocated two business/information architects and the IT division eight IT architects. The task assignments are indicated below.

The function of the enterprise architect consists of:

— the elaboration and maintenance of the enterprise architecture (EA for B-Sure Bank),

— the elaboration and maintenance of architectural principles and models for B-Sure Bank shared facilities,

— the maintenance and promotion of the B-Sure Bank architectural approach,

— the periodic review of divisional project and asset portfolios to ensure mutual consistency and the reporting of these reviews to the board of directors,

— the ensuring of harmony between business divisions and the IT division.

The function of the business/information architect comprises:

— the elaboration and maintenance of the domain architectures (in the areas of business and information architecture) required to steer and supervise business changes in their own divisions,

— the collaboration with IT architects in developing project-start architectures by means of which architecture is integrated into projects,

— the monitoring of projects to ensure that they comply with the architecture,

— the maintenance of the relevant architecture principles and models in their own divisions insofar as business and information architecture is concerned,

— the assessment of the impact of enterprise architecture on the functions, processes and systems within their own divisions.

The IT architect function involves:

— the elaboration and maintenance of the technical domain architectures needed to facilitate business changes in the other divisions,

— the collaboration with business/information architects in developing project-start architectures by means of which architecture is integrated into business-division projects,

— the monitoring of projects to ensure that they comply with the technical architecture,

— the maintenance of the architectural principles and models relevant to the technical architecture,

— the assessment of the impact that enterprise architecture has on the technical infrastructure managed by the IT division at B-Sure Bank.

I am convinced that the new architecture distribution will further enhance the capacity of B-Sure Bank, and I look forward to receiving your decision.

With warm regards,
Arnold Hedges
Manager of Architecture

# APPENDIX 1
# ARCHITECTURE MATURITY MATRIX

## Introduction

The Architecture Maturity Matrix was introduced in Chapter 6. This instrument enables any organization wanting to professionalize its architectural practices to devote the right amount of attention to the right area at the right time. The Maturity Matrix helps you to recognize the appropriate steps for improvement in areas of the organization that have priority at any given time.

To identify the appropriate improvement steps, it is first necessary to assess the state of the organization in terms of the Maturity Matrix's 18 key areas. This appendix will help you to perform this assessment. This appendix identifies checkpoints for every level of each key area to determine whether an organization has attained the level in question.

If an organization does not satisfy all the checkpoints of a given level but the organization still wants to reach that level, some suggestions for improvement may be useful. We provide those suggestions for improvement in this appendix. They are explicitly intended as suggestions, and are neither exhaustive nor applicable to every situation. They are meant to be sources of inspiration derived from our experiences – you can extract whatever is useful and then supplement it with your own improvement activities.

To appreciate the structure of this appendix it is helpful to refer to the Architecture Maturity Matrix (Figure A1.1).

In the Maturity Matrix, the columns represent stages on the pathway of increasing maturity. The rows contain the 18 key areas. The letters in the matrix indicate the level of maturity at each stage. The step-by-step improvement progresses from left to right in the matrix.

Observe the following rules in applying the Maturity Matrix:

— An organization attains a level when all the checkpoints at that level and all preceding levels have been satisfied.

| Key area \ Stage | 0 | 1 | 2 | 3 | 4 | 5 | 6 | 7 | 8 | 9 | 10 | 11 | 12 | 13 |
|---|---|---|---|---|---|---|---|---|---|---|---|---|---|---|
| Development of architecture | | A | | | B | | | C | | | | | | |
| Use of architecture | | | A | | | B | | | | C | | | | |
| Alignment with business | | A | | | | B | | | | C | | | | |
| Alignment with the development process | | | A | | | | B | C | | | | | | |
| Alignment with operations | | | | A | | | B | | | C | | | | |
| Relationship to the as-is state | | | | A | | | | | B | | | | | |
| Roles and responsibilities | | | | A | | B | | | | C | | | | |
| Coordination of developments | | | | | | | A | | | B | | | | |
| Monitoring | | | | A | | B | | C | | D | | | | |
| Quality management | | | | | | | | A | | B | | | C | |
| Maintenance of the architectural process | | | | | | | | A | B | | C | | | |
| Maintenance of architectural deliverables | | | | | A | | | | B | | | | C | |
| Commitment and motivation | | A | | | | | B | C | | | | | | |
| Architectural roles and training | | | | A | | B | | C | | | D | | | |
| Use of an architectural method | | | | A | | | | | | B | | | | C |
| Consultation | | | A | | B | | | | C | | | | | |
| Architectural tools | | | | | | | | A | | | B | | | C |
| Budgeting and planning | | | | A | | | | | | | B | C | | |

*Figure A1.1* **Architecture Maturity Matrix**

— An organization achieves a stage of maturity when all the levels at that stage and at all previous stages have been attained.

In this appendix, the notion of architecture is being interpreted broadly as a consistent set of principles and models that give direction to the design and realization of processes, organizational structures, information, applications and technical infrastructure of an organization. If an organization possesses such principles and models, we consider those to be a part of architecture, even if they are not identified as such by the organization.

In the context of this appendix, the term architectural process refers to all the activities involved in making and maintaining architectures, as well as aligning them with such other processes as planning and control, decision making, development and operations and maintenance.

It is furthermore assumed that Development with(out) Architecture is performed in projects, which may be either in-house or outsourced. These projects can involve the development and implementation of IT solutions in either customized or standardized packages, as well as updates to processes and organizational structures.

Individual sections devoted to each of the key areas in the Architecture Maturity Matrix are presented in the order that the areas are listed in the matrix, beginning with *development of architecture*. The levels (A, B, C and D) in each of the areas will be discussed. Checkpoints and suggestions for improvement are provided for each level. These can be used to establish where you are in terms of your own situation and how you might improve it. The suggestions for improvement can also be used to take advantage of opportunities in your organization apart from the levels you are currently working on.

## Development of Architecture

### • Level A: Architecture undertaken in projects

The development of architecture is undertaken as a project with a sponsor, a pre-defined final result and an end date.

*Checkpoints*

— Is an architecture only developed if there is a sponsor for it?

— Is a Project Plan drafted before an architecture is developed?

*Suggestions for improvement*

— *Arrange for a sponsor.* Ensure that the primary sponsor for any architecture being developed is explicitly indicated. Take the task of finding a sponsor seriously. This means that the sponsor should be actively involved in the development of the architecture.

— *Develop architecture according to a plan.* Establish the architectural product that is needed. Then make a Project Plan for the development of the architecture. Implement the plan as a project. Include the elements mentioned in Chapter 4 in the plan: sponsor, purpose and target group, orientation, use of the architecture, scope and content of the architecture, relationship with the other architectures, approach, stakeholders, approval and maintenance of the architecture.

— *Arrange for coaching.* Where necessary, obtain coaching, mentoring or training for your own architects from experienced architects elsewhere.

### • Level B: Architecture as a continuous process

Architecture must be kept up to date, since the world is not standing still. Once developed, architectures should be put into operations and maintained. There should be some release procedure or a form of release management for architectural products.

*Checkpoints*

— Is the development of architecture viewed as a continuous process?

— Is the architecture kept up to date?

— Is there some form of release management?

*Suggestions for improvement*

— *Set up release management for architecture.* To begin with, provide each architectural product with a version number, version history, owner, date and status. When there are new developments that require the architecture to be modified, a new version with updated version data is issued. Additionally, consider establishing review and acceptance procedures.

— *Demonstrate architectural coherence.* Demonstrate the coherence between architectures by making the relationships among the various architectures in the organization apparent. The DYA framework can be used for this purpose. By positioning all the architectures in this framework, it is possible to reveal the elements common to several architectures.

- **Level C: Architecture as a facilitation process**

It is clear to all stakeholders that the sole purpose for developing architecture is to support the changes needed to achieve business goals. The goal and function of every architecture is apparent right from the start.

*Checkpoints*

— Prior to developing architecture, has it been established who the sponsor is?

— Prior to developing architecture, has it been established who will profit from the results?

— Besides the architects, are other parties involved in the development of architecture (for example, business managers, administrators, developers, production employees)?

*Suggestions for improvement*

— *Actively involve stakeholders.* Actively involve stakeholders in the development of architecture to an extent corresponding to the degree of their interest. Describe the role of the stakeholders in the Project Plan for the relevant architecture.

## Use of Architecture

- **Level A: Architecture used informatively**

The architecture gives a clear picture of where the organization wants to be and inspires it to strive after this to-be state. This vision is endorsed by management. All employees have access to the architectural products.

*Checkpoints*

- Is there an architecture that management recognizes as such?

- Does the architecture give a clear indication of what the organization wants?

- Is the architecture accessible to all employees?

*Suggestions for improvement*

- *Publish the architecture.* Ensure that the existing architectures are brought to the attention of the organization. Publish the architecture on the intranet. To raise the profile in a more active manner, make presentations to specific target groups. Only develop architecture that fits in with the vision of where the organization ultimately wants to go.

- **Level B: Architecture used to steer content**

The architecture is, in fact, used to steer the choices made in projects. Projects must comply with the architecture.

*Checkpoints*

- Is the architecture used to give direction (in advance) to business and IT developments?

- Are projects clear about the parts of the architecture that apply to them?

- Does the architecture provide concrete guidelines that can be used by projects?

*Suggestions for improvement*

- *Implement project-start architecture.* Supply each project with a project-start architecture. Project-start architectures are formulated so that they are accessible, understandable and applicable to projects. Project-start architectures also provide the frameworks that give effective direction to the decisions made in projects.

- **Level C: Architecture integrated into the organization**

Architecture is an integral component of organizational governance. It is an important factor in decision-making processes.

*Checkpoints*

- Is architecture used in the organization's decision-making processes?

- Is architecture incorporated into the organization's planning and control cycle?

- Is the architecture based on the vision of senior management?

*Suggestions for improvement*

- *Incorporate architecture into the planning and control cycle.* Incorporate the role of architecture into the organization's planning and budgeting cycle. This means that, in formulating annual plans, architectural factors are considered when projects and programs are being selected. In practice, this mostly occurs by involving a member of the architect team in planning.

---

## Alignment with Business

- **Level A: Architecture tested for compatibility with business goals**

Architectural choices are supported by establishing a direct relationship to the business goals.

*Checkpoints*

- Is there a clear relationship between the architecture and the organization's business goals?

- Is the architecture evaluated in terms of the business goals?

*Suggestions for improvement*

- *Explain the basis of the architecture.* Examine the existing architecture and relate choices and agreements to the business strategy and goals (to the extent that this has not already been done). The DYA architectural framework can help you here. If such a relationship cannot be established, take a very critical look at the architectural principles and models. Frequently, choices and agreements are made about architecture without any reference to business goals and requirements. As a consequence, the choices are constantly being questioned.

- **Level B: Architectural process geared to business goals**

The development of architecture is geared to the business goals of the organization. The decision to work on architecture is completely determined by the business changes in store.

*Checkpoints*

- Do architects and business representatives meet regularly?

- Is the development of architecture concerned with concrete business goals?

- In developing architecture, is it generally clear which business goal is involved?

*Suggestions for improvement*

- *Set up account management for business.* Initiate dialogue with business managers and their representatives, such as the information managers of the business units. This can be done by allocating business domains to the architects. The architects build up a lasting, structural relationship with their "accounts." They come to know what is going on inside the given business domain, where the needs are and how architecture can contribute to the achievement of the business goals.

- **Level C: The architectural process is an integral component of business**

Architectural thinking is an essential constituent of the organization. Architects and business managers together participate in the Strategic Dialogue. Architecture offers concrete support for the strategic discussions of the organization.

*Checkpoints*

- Are there regular discussions with business when architecture is being developed?

- Does business feel that it is involved in the architectural process?

- Is architecture regarded as a strategic factor by senior management?

*Suggestions for improvement*

- *Involve architecture in the pre-project phase (Strategic Dialogue).* To begin with, collaborate with business management to determine what the added value of architecture has to be for the organization. Based on this determination, establish the added value of architecture in the business discussions leading up to the initiation of projects in formulating the business cases, for example. This added value is mostly to be found in the rapid provision of insight concerning the consequences of choices and the manner of achieving business goals.

- *Set up issue management.* Make an agreement with the business managers that the architect team will take on the task of monitoring difficult issues. This means that the architect team will prepare and coordinate the handling and resolution of these issues with business management, and incorporate the results into policy. Of course, the resolved issues are also immediately converted into architecture.

## Alignment with the Development Process

### • Level A: Ad hoc

There is some awareness in projects that frameworks exist and that work is being performed in accordance with them. Here and there, projects even ask for such frameworks.

*Checkpoints*

- Are there projects that take architecture into account?

- Are questions about the architecture coming from projects?

*Suggestions for improvement*

- *Discuss the role of architecture with project managers.* With the project managers, discuss what the relationship is between architecture and projects, why architecture is important and what this means for project execution. For example, have an architect discuss this at a project managers' work meeting.

- **Level B: Structural**

Projects are assumed to work within architectural frameworks. Architecture is a component of the standard working procedure for projects.

*Checkpoints*

- As a rule, do projects comply with architecture?

- Does architecture have a place in the standard development process?

- Do the architects pay explicit attention to the usability of the architecture in projects?

- Are standards and norms used in the development process?

*Suggestions for improvement*

- *Embed architecture in the project method.* Many organizations have a method for working on projects. This can be a standard method, such as PRINCE2, but it can also be the organization's own procedure as laid out in a project manual. Give architecture a place in this procedure by literally writing it into the standard project work procedure. The role of architecture is therefore explicitly added to the project method.

- **Level C: Interactive**

There is an interactive dialogue between architects and projects in which the architects support projects in their use of architectural frameworks and projects provide feedback on the quality and applicability of the architecture.

*Checkpoints*

- Does feedback from the development process to the architectural process occur on a regular basis?

- Do the architects help the developers focus the general architectural principles on their specific situation?

- Do the developers actively help with the development of architecture?

- Have processes been established so that, in special cases, in a deliberate and controlled way development can deviate from the architecture?

*Suggestions for improvement*

- *Set up account management for the development process.* Initiate regular meetings between members of the architect team and representatives from system development. The purpose of these meetings is to ensure good collaboration between architects and projects.

- *Collectively develop project-start architecture.* Have architects and project teams together develop the project-start architecture, which is architecture focused on the situation of a specific project.

- *Introduce the management letter.* Occasionally stakeholders will agree, after discussion and by consensus, to allow a project to deviate from the architecture. Use the management letter as a tool to record and distribute these agreements. The agreements described in the management letter determine how the deviation will be handled and if/how a structural solution will be realized. The management letter can also be a component in a project-start architecture.

## Alignment with Operations

- **Level A: Ad hoc**

There is some awareness that, on the one hand, operations and maintenance issues (such as the ability to install, learn and restore) must be considered when making architectural choices and, on the other hand, operations and maintenance must also comply with the architectural frameworks.

*Checkpoints*

- Do administrators take architecture into account?

- Are Operations and Maintenance issues dealt with in the architecture?

*Suggestions for improvement*

— *Discuss the role of architecture with administrators.* With the administrators, discuss what the relationship is between architecture and O&M, why architecture is important and what this means for performing operations and maintenance. For example, have an architect discuss this at an administrators' work meeting.

- **Level B: Structural**

Administrators are assumed to work within the frameworks of the architecture. It is standard practice to consider O&M issues when developing architecture.

*Checkpoints*

— Is it standard for Operations and Maintenance to be a key consideration when developing architecture?

— Are administrators required to comply with architecture?

*Suggestions for improvement*

— *Integrate architecture into operations and maintenance procedures.* Incorporate the role of architecture into operations. For example, this means that change requests must be subjected to an architectural review.

- **Level C: Interactive**

There is an interactive dialogue between architects and administrators in which the architects support the administrators in their use of architectural frameworks and the administrators provide feedback on the quality and applicability of the architecture.

*Checkpoints*

— Does feedback from administrators to the architectural process occur on a regular basis?

— Are administrators involved in the development of architecture?

— Are there guidelines concerning the maintenance of systems that were developed without architecture?

*Suggestions for improvement*

— *Set up account management for operations and maintenance.* Initiate regular meetings between members of the architect team and administrator representatives. These meetings have, among other things, the aim of taking an inventory of the administrators' architectural wants.

---

## Relationship to the As-Is State

### • Level A: Attention to the as-is state

The architecture does not only sketch the desired target state but devotes a great deal of attention to the current state (existing processes, organizational structures, information, applications and technical infrastructure) and the manner of dealing with it.

*Checkpoints*

— In the architecture, is attention paid to the as-is state (existing processes, organizational structures, information, applications and technical infrastructure)?

— Has a policy been formulated concerning the as-is state (existing processes, organizational structures, information, applications and technical infrastructure)?

*Suggestions for improvement*

— *Formulate policy for as-is state.* Develop a vision about the future of the current state of processes, organizational structures, information, applications and technical infrastructure. Based on this vision, formulate concrete guidelines on how to proceed. These guidelines indicate the conditions under which parts of the current state should be replaced or updated.

— *Set up asset management.* Map out the entire set of IT assets (applications and technical infrastructure) and subject it to asset management. Take such matters into account as the functional and technical value of applications, life-cycle management, costs and use. The objective of asset management is to enable IT investment decisions to be made in a thoughtful manner.

- **Level B: Attention to migration**

The architecture provides insight into the possibilities of migrating from the as-is to the to-be state.

*Checkpoints*

- Does the architecture indicate a relationship between the as-is and the to-be state?

- Does the architecture suggest any guidelines concerning migration (how to move from the as-is to the to-be state)?

*Suggestions for improvement*

- *Draft a migration scenario.* Sketch the possibilities of migrating from the as-is to the to-be state based on architecture. Include these possibilities as a standard component of the architecture. It has already been stated in Chapter 4 that advice on the effects of architecture should be a component of the architecture.

---

## Roles and Responsibilities

- **Level A: Responsibility for architectural content assigned**

Responsibility has been assigned for the architectural content. The architecture has an owner.

*Checkpoints*

- Has the responsibility for the architectural content been explicitly assigned to someone?

- Does the architecture have an official status in the organization?

*Suggestions for improvement*

- *Obtain a mandate for architecture.* Ask senior management to express their commitment to architectural practices and to explicitly assign the responsibility for the architecture.

- *Draw up a table of responsibilities.* Construct a table of responsibilities in which architecture-related tasks are matched with the various functions in the organization. Indicate the person responsible for each task as well as the person who performs it. For this purpose, use such techniques as RACI (Responsible, Accountable, Consulting, Informed) or RAEW (Responsibility, Authority, Expertise, Work).

— *Set up an architecture board.* Create an architecture board to formally approve architectural products and to provide an escalation platform to deal with deviations from the architecture. Members of the architectural board are to be recruited from the senior management of both business and IT.

## • Level B: Management responsible for the architectural process

The management-level responsibility for the process of developing architecture and using it in the organization has been assigned.

*Checkpoints*

— Has someone at the management level been assigned responsibility for architecture?

— Has an owner of the architectural processes been appointed?

*Suggestions for improvement*

— *Appoint a process owner for architecture.* Assign ownership of the architectural process. The process owner of architecture is not only responsible for the processes in which architecture is developed but also for its alignment with other processes, such as the development and maintenance processes. The process owner is responsible for the effectiveness and efficiency of the architectural processes.

## • Level C: Senior management responsible for the effect of architecture

Architecture is included in the portfolio of one of the senior managers. The consequences of architectural practices are evaluated.

*Checkpoints*

— Has someone at the senior management level been assigned responsibility for architecture?

— Is architecture also the responsibility of business management?

— Has the person (or body) responsible for architecture been made accountable for the extent to which architecture contributes to the business goals?

*Suggestions for improvement*

— *Allocate final responsibility for architecture.* Ensure that senior management is actually involved in architecture, especially on the business side. Ensure that the ultimate responsibility for the architecture is allocated to the portfolio of a business manager.

---

## Coordination of Developments

### • Level A: Steering the content in each project

The architecture is used to steer the content of projects insofar as their delineation and high-level design choices are concerned. Before a project is initiated, an examination is made of how it will fit into current and planned projects.

*Checkpoints*

— Is the architecture used as a guiding principle in making design choices for individual projects?

— Is architecture used to prevent projects from having to reinvent the wheel?

— Is architecture used to prevent projects from doing work that has already been done?

*Suggestions for improvement*

— *Make project-start architecture mandatory.* The project-start architecture makes architecture accessible to projects and makes it possible to steer their content. Not a single project is begun without project-start architecture.

### • Level B: Coherence among projects

Architecture is used to actively monitor the entire range of projects. Projects are delineated on the basis of architecture, and the results of the various projects are coordinated with each other.

*Checkpoints*

— Is architecture used to achieve coherence among projects?

— Is architecture used to distribute development activities among projects?

*Suggestions for improvement*

— *Embed architecture in project-portfolio management.* If a form of portfolio management exists, which would typically be financially oriented, introduce some architectural requirements into it. These will be specifically concerned with the coherence among projects. Collective or infrastructural elements should be included in collective projects. A rudimentary form of enterprise architecture is required to give shape to such activity.

---

## *Monitoring*

### • **Level A: Reactive monitoring**

Projects are reviewed to ensure compliance with architecture.

*Checkpoints*

— Is any consideration given to architecture in project progress reports?

— Are projects checked to ensure compliance with architecture?

— Does non-compliance with architecture have any consequences for the project manager or sponsor?

*Suggestions for improvement*

— *Implement an architectural review.* Schedule testing at points along the system development trajectory and test a project for compliance with architectural commitments. In addition to testing at the start of the project, test at other appropriate moments, like the delivery of the functional and technical design and the acceptance of the business solution. Link up with any feedback or testing mechanisms that may already exist (review procedures, go/no go moments, progress reports). If there are no testing mechanisms, an instrument such as a building permit may be used.

### • **Level B: Proactive monitoring**

Proactive efforts are made to ensure that projects comply with the architecture.

*Checkpoints*

- Are any control instruments being used to enforce compliance with the architecture (for example: building permits)?

- Do architects participate in design phases and definition studies?

- Are proactive efforts made to ensure that projects comply with architecture (for example: architecture promotion activities, relationship building with project managers, participation in project kick-offs)?

*Suggestions for improvement*

- *Implement project coaching.* Have an architect coach a project from its initiation or kick-off to its completion. The architect advises the project about architectural concerns and indicates how the project can comply with the architecture. Ultimately, the project decisions are made by the project manager and sponsor (with an escalation procedure in case of risky or unjustified deviations from the architecture). Project coaching can be implemented project by project, beginning with the most strategic projects.

- **Level C: Embedded monitoring**

Compliance with architecture is a standard component of project execution and is embedded in work procedures.

*Checkpoints*

- Is compliance with architecture a component of the project assignment?

- Is it a given that projects will comply with architecture?

*Suggestions for improvement*

- *Embed the compliance with architecture in the project method.* Make compliance with architecture a standard component of the project method. Many organizations have a standard method, such as PRINCE2. Indicate how monitoring compliance with architecture is incorporated into the project method.

- **Level D: Integrated monitoring**

Compliance with architecture is an integral component of enterprise governance.

*Checkpoints*

- Is architecture used to monitor the coherence of business and IT developments?

- Is compliance with architecture included in the organization's planning and control cycle?

*Suggestions for improvement*

- *Include the monitoring of architecture in the planning and control cycle.* Including architecture in the organization's planning and control cycle means that compliance with architecture is incorporated in the testing of annual plans. In practice, this mostly occurs by involving a member of the architect team in the evaluation (audit interviews) of the annual plans.

---

## Quality Management

- **Level A: Retrospective validation**

Developed architectures are validated in the best possible way. Questions are asked about the choices made, their suitability given the strategy and business goals of the organization and their effectiveness in delivering the intended benefits.

*Checkpoints*

- Are efforts made to validate the architecture in one manner or another?

- Are standards of quality identified for the architecture?

*Suggestions for improvement*

- *Establish an architectural review procedure.* Set up a review procedure to ensure that architectural products are reviewed by all the relevant stakeholders in the organization. Using a review matrix, it is possible to establish in advance the parties who should review architectural products.

- **Level B: Quality process developed**

A process has been developed to ensure the quality of architecture.

*Checkpoints*

- — Is attention systematically focused on the quality of the architectural process?

- — Is there an architectural quality program?

*Suggestions for improvement*

- — *Audit architecture.* Establish the quality requirements that the architecture must satisfy (both in terms of its process and content). Have audits regularly conducted in order to ascertain whether these requirements have been satisfied.

- **Level C: Embedded quality policy**

The assurance of architectural quality is a part of the organization's integral quality policy.

*Checkpoints*

- — Is the quality of architecture a part of the organization's overarching quality policy?

- — Is there a structural provision that focuses attention on the consequences of architectural practices (for example: the extent to which architectural practices contribute to the achievement of strategic business goals)?

- — In considering the quality of architecture, is any thought given to the relationship of architecture to other processes in the organization (for example: strategy formulation processes, development processes)?

*Suggestions for improvement*

- — *Include architectural processes in the quality system.* Include architectural processes in the organization's overall quality system. If there is no overall quality system, the architecture process can perhaps be used as a pilot to set up such a system. The objective of a quality system is to structurally evaluate and improve the architectural process.

## Maintenance of the Architectural Process

- **Level A: Maintenance performed in a fragmented manner**

It is recognized that the architecture process must be maintained.

*Checkpoints*

- Has the architectural process been described?

- Is the architectural process known to the organization?

- Has it ever been verified if the architectural process is still sufficient?

*Suggestions for improvement*

- *Conduct an assessment.* Conduct an assessment of the current state of affairs in the architectural process. The Architecture Maturity Matrix can be used for this purpose.

- *Describe the architectural processes.* Describe the architectural processes, such as the establishment and maintenance of architecture, the formalization of architectural products, the role of architecture in projects and maintenance, and the role of architecture in the pre-project phase. Include this in an architectural handbook.

- **Level B: Maintenance procedures are established**

Procedures have been established to maintain the architectural process.

*Checkpoints*

- Have maintenance procedures been established for the architectural process?

- Has maintenance of the architectural process been assigned within the organization?

- Are changes to the architectural process immediately communicated to stakeholders?

*Suggestions for improvement*

- *Establish a maintenance procedure for the architectural process.* Establish procedures to deal with changes to the architectural process. The aim of these is to actively maintain the architectural process and to keep it up to date.

- **Level C: Continuous process improvement**

The architectural process is regularly scrutinized and improvements are made on the basis of findings.

*Checkpoints*

- Is the architectural process evaluated at regular intervals?

- Is there a mechanism in place for submitting proposals to improve the architectural process?

- Do proposed improvements regularly result in actual adjustments to the architectural process?

*Suggestions for improvement*

- *Implement assessment and improvement cycle.* Establish a system in which assessments of the architectural process are regularly made. Ensure that the resulting proposals for improvement, along with any other suggestions for improvement that may occasionally arise, are evaluated according to a standard procedure and result in the necessary changes to the architectural process. Publish, communicate and implement these modifications.

---

## Maintenance of Architectural Deliverables

- **Level A: Maintenance is performed in a fragmented manner**

At set times, checks are performed on the architectures to ensure that they are still up to date. If this proves not to be the case, maintenance is carried out.

*Checkpoints*

- Has it ever been verified that the architecture is still up to date?

- Have outdated components been removed from the architecture?

- Has a new version of the architecture ever been issued?

*Suggestions for improvement*

— *Update architecture.* Examine the existing architectures. Are the principles and models still current? Are there any inconsistencies? In making these evaluations, constantly ask whether the architecture continues to serve the current business goals. Eliminate any elements that have become outdated or redundant, and adjust the architecture to meet current requirements. A framework, such as the DYA architecture framework, is a handy tool for this task.

- **Level B: Maintenance procedures are established**

Procedures have been established to keep architectural products up-to-date.

*Checkpoints*

— Has a maintenance procedure been established for architectural products?

— Is there a change management procedure in place for architectural products (a procedure for making changes to architectural products)?

— Is maintenance of architectural products one of the tasks mentioned in the architect's job description?

— Are changes to the architecture immediately communicated to all stakeholders?

*Suggestions for improvement*

— *Establish a maintenance procedure for architectural products.* Establish procedures for making changes to architecture (change management), for including architectural artifacts in the total architectural package and for maintaining the consistency of this totality. The aim is to actively maintain the architecture as a whole and to keep it up to date. A framework, such as the DYA architecture framework, is a handy tool for this task.

- **Level C: A maintenance policy exists**

A policy has been formulated concerning the manner in which architectural products are maintained. This policy is based on views about the quality assurance of the architectural products.

*Checkpoints*

— Is there a policy on the maintenance of architectural products?

— Are distinctions made in the ways of maintaining various architectural products?

*Suggestions for improvement*

— *Develop a maintenance policy.* Formulate a policy indicating how the maintenance of the various architectures is to be handled. This can, for example, indicate the architectures that are actively maintained, the times when such maintenance occurs and the individual(s) who perform(s) it.

---

## Commitment and Motivation

- **Level A: Allocation of budget and time**

Time and money are committed to architecture for the benefit of an architect team and/or an architectural project.

*Checkpoints*

— Does management regard architecture as important?

— Are money and time allocated to architecture?

*Suggestions for improvement*

— *Bring architecture to the attention of management.* Convince management of the value that architecture adds to the organization. Ask management to openly acknowledge architecture's value in both words and actions.

— *Obtain a budget.* Make a budget available. This can occur by explicitly including the role of architecture in annual plans or budget proposals or by earmarking time and/or money for it.

- **Level B: Architecture integrated into the processes of change**

Management recognizes and openly acknowledges that architecture is an indispensable part of the management and implementation of change.

*Checkpoints*

- Do business and IT management openly acknowledge architecture to be an indispensable part of business and IT projects?

- Do the guidelines concerning time, money and quality given by management to projects indicate that compliance with architecture is regarded as important?

- Are chapters on architecture included in the project plans?

- Do the organization's employees place any value on architecture?

*Suggestions for improvement*

- *Have management make the case for architecture.* Together with management, evaluate the value added by architecture and commit managers to the open support of it.

- *Include compliance with architecture in the project assignment.* Make compliance with architecture a standard component of the project assignment. While the project method describes how a project is executed, the project assignment indicates what the results of the project are to be.

- **Level C: Continuous architectural improvement accepted by organization**

Among management, there is a wide recognition that architecture is of strategic importance and that continuous attention to the quality of architectural practices is justified.

*Checkpoints*

- Are architects supported by management to continuously improve the architectural process?

- Does the organization supply regular feedback on the architectural process?

*Suggestions for improvement*

- *Involve the organization in the improvement trajectory.* Do not undertake a series of improvements on your own but keep the organization informed about progress. For instance, a customer satisfaction survey can be conducted in order to support the launch of improvement initiatives.

## *Architectural Roles and Training*

- **Level A: Role recognized**

The architect's role is recognized in the organization.

*Checkpoints*

- Does the role of architect exist in the organization?

*Suggestions for improvement*

- *Set up an architect team.* Assign a number of employees the role of architect, whether or not on a full-time basis. Adopt a principle requiring part-time architects to spend a minimum of 16 hours a week on architectural activities. If desired, the architects can be coached by experienced architects from outside the organization, either individually or in group training sessions.

- **Level B: Role described**

The architect's tasks and responsibilities are clearly described.

*Checkpoints*

- Have the architect's tasks and responsibilities been defined?

*Suggestions for improvement*

- *Describe the role of the architect.* Formally establish the architect's tasks and responsibilities and ensure that this role is approved at the management level.

- *Draft a service catalogue.* To make the added value of the architect team clear to the organization and to indicate the services that architects provide to the organization, compile a service catalogue for the team.

- **Level C: Role supported**

The architects are supported in the performance of their tasks and responsibilities with training, tools and a platform for the exchange of best practices.

*Checkpoints*

- Are the architects provided with methods and tools?

— Are there any training courses for the architects?

— Is there any provision for the exchange of best practices?

*Suggestions for improvement*

— *Professionalize the role of the architect.* Create an environment that nurtures and promotes professionalism. Architects have the resources that they need, the exchange of best practices is facilitated and training or coaching is provided.

## • Level D: Role valued

The architect's role is recognized and valued. Employees can have a career in architecture.

*Checkpoints*

— Are architects given the opportunity to be certified?

— Is there a training program for architects?

— Is there a career path for architects?

*Suggestions for improvement*

— *Remunerate the architect and recognize the role of the architect.* Provide architects with a career path and give them the opportunity to distinguish themselves. Enable them to become certified and to make a career of architecture (with appropriate remuneration). Facilitate their ongoing education.

---

## Use of an Architectural Method

## • Level A: Project specific

The establishment of architecture is preceded by the establishment of an applicable method. This can vary from architecture to architecture.

*Checkpoints*

— Is a Project Plan developed for each architectural project?

— Is the method defined for an architectural assignment actually applied?

— Does the method applied in an architectural assignment distinguish among the various aspects involved (for example: processes, data and applications)?

*Suggestions for improvement*

— *Establish a method in an architectural Project Plan.* Define the method for developing architecture in an architectural Project Plan. The method describes the results that will be delivered and the activities required for this purpose. Describe the results as accurately as possible. Make distinctions among the various aspects (for example: processes, data, applications), forms (principles, policy directives, models) and/or perspectives (enterprise architecture, domain architecture, project-start architecture).

- **Level B: Organization generic**

The organization employs a standard methodology in developing architecture.

*Checkpoints*

— Is a formalized generic architectural methodology used in the organization?

— Is the generic architectural methodology adopted in every architectural project?

— In executing architectural projects, are any deviations from the generic architectural methodology substantiated and documented?

*Suggestions for improvement*

— *Implement an architectural method.* Implement an organization-wide architectural method. This means that agreements are reached on the ways of differentiating architectures, the manner in which architectures are documented and how they are developed. These can, for example, be recorded in an architectural handbook.

- **Level C: Organizationally optimizing R&D activities**

The method of developing architectures is regularly evaluated and, where necessary, adjusted.

*Checkpoints*

— Is there a structured process for gathering feedback on the generic architectural methodology?

— Is the generic methodology subject to structural maintenance and innovation (R&D)?

*Suggestions for improvement*

— *Evaluate the architectural method.* Set up a mechanism to periodically examine the architectural method and, where necessary, adjust it. Stakeholders obviously must be informed about adjustments.

## Consultation

- **Level A: Internal architectural meetings**

The architects regularly hold internal meetings in which experiences are exchanged and content issues discussed.

*Checkpoints*

— Are there regular architect team meetings?

— Are the agreements made within the architect team properly documented?

*Suggestions for improvement*

— *Institute architect meetings.* Institute a periodic (weekly or biweekly) internal architect meeting. The primary purpose of this meeting is the transfer and exchange of knowledge. At these meetings, new developments can be reported and discussed, and new issues raised. Compile a decision and action list based on each meeting and distribute it.

— *Organize workshops.* Besides the periodic meeting, practice has proven it is extremely refreshing and useful to hold, once in a while (for example, once a year) a one- or two-day workshop somewhere off the organization's premises. This allows the architect team to reflect and to examine the performance and effectiveness of the architecture function. Besides strengthening team spirit, significant improvement initiatives can emerge from this exercise.

- **Level B: Meetings with sponsors and users of architecture**

There are regular meetings with sponsors and users of architecture about the function of architecture in the organization.

*Checkpoints*

— Do regular meetings occur with the sponsors of architectural projects?

— Do regular meetings occur with the developers who (are to) work in compliance with the architecture?

— Is a record kept of the agreements made with the sponsor of the architecture?

— Is a record kept of the agreements made with the developers who (are to) work in compliance with architecture?

*Suggestions for improvement*

— *Conduct a Stakeholder Inventory.* Identify the stakeholders of architecture, what their interests are, what roles they play insofar as architecture is concerned and how they can be involved. This inventory can be used to determine the appropriate manner of communicating with stakeholders.

— *Draw up a Communication Matrix.* Construct a Communication Matrix in which a record of communication with each target group (group stakeholders and interested parties) is kept, indicating what architectural topic will be discussed, when, how and by whom. In this way, the Communication Matrix constitutes an instrument in which all communications concerning architecture are planned and monitored. In planning communication activities, it is extremely important to have a clear idea about what the objective is. In addition, the timing of the actions is important. Waiting too long before communicating to stakeholders leads to an ivory-tower situation. Communicating too soon creates the risk that expectations may be aroused that cannot soon be fulfilled.

— *Establish an architectural community.* Establish a community in which architects and stakeholders talk about issues in an informal manner. The aim of the architectural community is to involve people in the organization with architecture and, at the same time, to create a sounding board for the architects. The issues can involve both the content and the process of architecture. At a later stage, the community can be given a more formal status. See the improvement suggestions for "Set up an architectural platform" in the following level.

- **Level C: All-encompassing discussions about the quality of the architectural processes in the organization**

In meetings with the most important stakeholders, consideration is given to possible or desirable improvements to the architecture function.

*Checkpoints*

— Are there regular meetings with the sponsors and users of architecture at which to discuss proposals for improving the applied architectural methodology and the architectural processes?

— Is a record kept of the agreements made to improve the architectural methodology and processes?

*Suggestions for improvement*

— *Set up an architectural platform.* Set up an architectural platform in which architects and stakeholders can come together and, in a formal manner, discuss issues and make decisions. The most important stakeholders are business managers, project managers and IT management (system maintenance and development). The issues can involve both the content and the process of architecture. If necessary, work groups can be instructed to research and elaborate certain elements.

---

## Architectural tools

- **Level A: Ad hoc and product based**

Tools are used in a fragmentary manner to support architectural practices. An example would be a process management tool for developing process architectures.

*Checkpoints*

— Are tools used to support architectural practices?

*Suggestions for improvement*

— *Run a pilot using architectural tools.* Undertake a pilot project using a tool to support the development and maintenance of architectures. Begin with a tool for the aspect or area in which the need for a tool is greatest (for example: process architecture). Use the pilot project to acquire experience with the tool and to determine the architectures for which the tool may be useful.

- **Level B: Structural and process based**

The architects all use the same tools. These tools not only support the development of individual architectures but also the process of developing and maintaining them.

*Checkpoints*

— Do the architects use the same tools?

— Is the management of architectural tools explicitly assigned to someone in the organization?

— Do the architectural tools support the architectural process?

*Suggestions for improvement*

— *Implement architectural tools.* Select the architectural tool(s) that best supports the architect's work and implement it/them organization-wide in such a manner that the use of the tool is integrated into the organization's architectural process.

- **Level C: Integration of tools**

The architects are supported by an integrated set of tools for performing various functions, where the integration of the tools ensures the overall consistency of the architectural artifacts.

*Checkpoints*

— Are the employed architectural tools integrated in one way or another?

— Can the architectural tools be used to ensure the consistency of architectural artifacts?

*Suggestions for improvement*

— *Implement an integrated toolkit.* Implement an integrated toolkit that not only develops various architectures but, given the integration of the tools, ensures architectural consistency.

## *Budgeting and Planning*

### • Level A: Project specific

A planning procedure precedes the development of architecture. Adherence to the plan is monitored throughout the development trajectory.

*Checkpoints*

— Are plans made for architectural projects?

— Is the progress in an architectural project monitored?

*Suggestions for improvement*

— *Make plans for architectural projects.* Formulate a plan for architectural projects. This plan at least includes an estimate of the project duration, the human and other resources required, and time frames for the completion of project components and milestones.

### • Level B: Organization generic

There is a standard budgeting and planning methodology for the development of architectures.

*Checkpoints*

— Is there a standard budgeting and planning methodology for architectural projects?

— In executing architectural projects, are any deviations from established budgets and plans documented and explained?

*Suggestions for improvement*

— *Implement a planning method.* Implement an organization-wide planning method. This means that a plan is always formulated for architectural projects in accordance with a prescribed set of standard activities, rules and guidelines for budgeting and planning.

## • Level C: Optimizing

The budgeting and planning of architectural projects is conducted in a systematic and professional manner with attention to the quality of the process.

*Checkpoints*

- Is there a systematic process for gathering feedback on the budgeting and planning method used for architectural projects?

- Is there any statistical data available on the budgets and plans for architectural projects executed in the past?

*Suggestions for improvement*

- *Evaluate architectural plans.* Collect data on planning and execution of previous architectural projects and use these empirical figures to professionalize the planning process.

---

## To Conclude

The employment of architecture involves many factors. In this appendix, we have defined 18 of them – each one with its own developmental path. That is too many for an organization to address all at once. The Architecture Maturity Matrix is an instrument to focus attention on specific areas, one at a time. Using the checkpoints it is possible to determine the current status of an organization. Mapping the organization onto the Maturity Matrix can identify the key areas to be emphasized in the near future and to what extent this should be done. The suggestions for improvement show the concrete actions that are appropriate in the given circumstances.

# APPENDIX 2
# THINKING ABOUT CHANGE IN FIVE DIFFERENT COLORS

## *Introduction*

The implementation of architecture represents a trajectory of change and must be approached as such. Fortunately, there is a great deal of literature available. Various change management approaches and theories have been developed. It is certainly worthwhile, in beginning a process of professionalization, to familiarize yourself with the field.

One approach that strongly appeals to us and that we want to share with you is De Caluwé and Vermaak's color model of thinking. In their book *Learning to Change* they use colors to represent the ways of thinking and acting that characterize an organization, organizational unit or person. They distinguish five such colors: yellow, blue, red, green and white. The most suitable manner of change depends upon the dominant color.

Yellow is an approach based on socio-political observations about organizations. Interests, conflicts and power all play important roles. Change is achieved when you get everyone pulling in the same direction.

Blue is characterized by the logical design and rational implementation of change. To a large extent, the path to results follows rational arguments that are planned and measured using indexes.

Red is centered on personal relationships. Change is accomplished by deploying, for example, such HRM instruments as evaluation and remuneration systems and assessments. People do something when they get something in return.

Green is based on learning, both by individuals and by the organization as a whole. Change occurs by placing motivated people in learning situations.

White characterizes a self-organization process that generates new structures and modes of behavior. People and organizations are continuously undergoing change.

This kaleidoscope can be used to examine architectural practices as well.

185

## The Colors of Change in Relation to Architecture

### The Yellow Look

Architecture should be viewed as part of the socio-political dynamic. Since it reproduces the collective vision of the organization, it is a means of getting everybody in step. Support is crucial. The development of architecture occurs by organizing workshops for all the stakeholders. One main architectural goal is to streamline discussions of content issues and, above all, to provide solutions. Architecture involves making agreements. By employing architecture, it becomes possible to discover and work toward common interests.

The underlying purpose of architecture is to achieve business goals. In doing this, the interests of the various business units are given serious consideration and weighed appropriately. Conflicting interests are recognized and resolved through negotiation. In this case, architecture helps to create win-win situations.

#### Appropriate Procedure

First of all, strive for a widely supported fundamental vision. What are the basic architectural principles? All parties should be involved in determining them. In the beginning, pay a great deal of attention to raising architecture's profile. The organization must recognize the importance of participating in this image-building exercise, as important decisions are made at this point. The focus is on workshops. Once the underlying vision is in place, examine its significance for the organization's work practices. All developments are immediately checked against this vision. If a development does not fit into it, a committee of representatives then determines what to do. Continued support from the entire organization remains a constant preoccupation. This requires such activities as regular stakeholder meetings.

### The Blue Look

Architecture is a control instrument. Its purpose is to tightly control the changes in an organization. Architecture ensures that project results are compatible with the greater whole. An important tool in this regard is the project-start architecture. Project planning can also be made more reliable with the help of architecture. With the help of architecture, decisions can be supported more clearly and on the basis of rational arguments. The architecture is developed by architects who have expertise and make decisions focused on business goals. The validity of the architecture is demonstrated using a means-ends hierarchy. The total set of projects is coordinated by some form of project-portfolio management.

## Appropriate Procedure

A project-based approach is used to develop architectural practices. The deliverables are defined: an initial version of the architecture, the maintenance processes, an updated project method, escalation mechanisms, etc. A project team undertakes to deliver these items. Once the project is completed, the next phase is initiated: the actual employment of the architecture. At that point, the developed processes are put into effect.

## The Red Look

Architecture is meant to improve collaboration and establish clearer goals. It is a vehicle to involve various disciplines in working toward certain results. Because architecture makes the relationships among things clear, work packages and personal targets can be coordinated with each other. The purpose of architecture is to ensure that employees are given clear targets on the basis of which they can be evaluated in a transparent manner and appropriately remunerated. An important part of the architecture is the organization architecture: the vision of how an enterprise has to be organized and what types of employees are required.

## Appropriate Procedure

Roles are defined at the start, along with responsibilities, architect duties and organizational positions. Tasks and responsibilities in all related areas are recorded in job descriptions. New job descriptions are established for the architect roles. New sorts of targets are formulated. Employees are personally informed of what working with architecture means for them personally and how it can be to their advantage (earning promotions, as a platform for good ideas, enabling new task assignments).

## The Green Look

Architecture provides an organization with a stepping stone to learning, development and innovation. Since the vision of how things must be done is incorporated into an architecture, this vision is stable and accessible to the entire organization. This stability and continuity means that employees can build upon knowledge acquired by others. Instead of continuously reinventing the wheel, it is possible to pick up where someone else has left off.

### Appropriate Procedure

Right from the start, working with architecture is presented as a shared learning process. The process begins with courses on *architectural practices*. Stakeholders from all branches of the organization are invited to attend. In this way, everyone is given a clear idea of what architecture is and why the organization wants it. Courses tailored to the various target groups are also organized. Presentations by external experts are held as well. The architects are stimulated to write for publication and to attend conferences (both as speakers and audience members). For the advanced architects, there is a biweekly master class on architecture in which experiences and best practices are exchanged. The architects are assisted by a coach.

## The White Look

Architecture is a response to the organization's collective expertise. By reflecting on strategic issues, architectural principles bubble to the surface more or less on their own. These are assembled into an architecture. New architectural principles will be created as the need arises. In this way, architecture is a mechanism that provides a place for employees' self-organization and their compulsion to innovate, while ensuring good results.

### Appropriate Procedure

The concept of architecture and its added value are brought up periodically for discussion. A watchful eye is kept on those individuals in the organization who tend to take up ideas and run with them a bit. When employees do this, they are observed in order to see what they accomplish. If subtle intervention is advisable, they are pointed in the right direction. The various architectural initiatives may be correlated in some way or another, without forcing cohesion. Intervention only occurs when conflicts arise that have a detrimental effect on the organization. Architectural practices are permitted to flourish without obstruction, but if architectural initiatives fail to get off the ground, the organization understands that to mean they are not ready to work with architecture. Architecture is not mandatory.

The color model of thinking is a handy tool with which to examine architecture from various perspectives. It illustrates the fact that people and business cultures can differ. An architect who takes such differences into account in his or her approach and communication practices will be more successful than one who fails to do so. It is therefore worthwhile to learn to recognize colors, to play with them and to act accordingly.

*Key aspect to ID. is understanding os. people + culture*

## Mismatching Colors

The following examples illustrate what can go wrong when there is an undetected mismatch of colors. The sketches concern situations in which there are differences in color between the architects and the rest of the organization – particularly management.

## A Blue Architect in a Yellow Organization

Tony Ashe is hired as an information consultant for the Concern IT department. One of his responsibilities is IT architecture. He has definite views on this subject, so the assignment is appropriate. Without delay, Tony begins to draft a well-conceived architectural document. After two months, it is ready. Tony takes it to his boss, Mark Templeton, in order to explain the next step in the process: the distribution of the architectural document and the establishment of review procedures for projects.

The meeting seems to go well. Mark appears to fall into line and says that he will draw up a distribution list, but then does not follow up on this discussion for two weeks. With some effort, Tony is able to arrange another meeting with Mark. It is certainly a good document; that's not the issue. They discuss the timing, other priorities, and sensitivities in the organization. The final word is that the document will not be distributed. The timing is just not right because all sorts of developments are going on, and there appears to be a reorganization in the works. They have to wait for that. Right now, the priority is for Concern IT to maintain its current position.

An IT day is organized for the business units in order to strengthen the relationship between Concern IT and the Business Units. Architecture is given a place on the agenda and Tony makes a presentation. He indicates that, besides an IT architecture, there should be a process architecture. One doesn't yet exist, so Tony proposes to make a start on it. He displays the architecture and says that those present will have to validate it. By the time he has reached this point in his presentation, he has long since lost his audience. After a little polite applause at the end of Tony's presentation, Mark states that, of course, some consideration must be given to precisely how to handle the architectural document. Although business will certainly not be burdened with it, it is certainly nice to have such a document to fall back on. Everyone nods politely and proceeds to the next item on the agenda.

Tony is bewildered. How could this happen? Hadn't he been asked to develop an architecture? And now it appears that no one was expecting it. They were all busy with their own positions and the forming of coalitions. Don't they see that huge opportunities for synergy will be lost to the company if they don't begin work on his architecture? Oh well! If they don't want to, they don't. He has done his job. The ball is now in management's court.

After a few months, a completely frustrated Tony leaves the company to go to work for a competitor that is looking for an IT architect.

## Green Architects in a Red Organization

The directors of the Volin Company, which has 450 employees, decide that there should be more structure in the company's IT practices. Until now, the departments have been able to directly approach someone they happen to know in IT and ask for changes or even new applications. Given the IT department's service-oriented outlook, IT has been quite willing to satisfy these requests. Gradually an uncontrolled proliferation of systems has evolved and no one knows any longer if or how they are interrelated. The directors have also heard about the problem of legacy, and want to avoid it. As a result, a number of senior IT specialists are given the assignment of developing architecture.

John Thorpe, Margaret Feldman and Berry Wiggins enthusiastically sit down to work. They have always been the first to learn something new. They read articles and books, attend conferences and register in courses at the Open University. They attempt to involve their colleagues in this learning process – not only colleagues in their own IT department but also those from other departments. They recognize that architecture is not something confined to the IT department alone and that collaboration with business is crucial. Unfortunately, collaboration and learning has not always been well received. People are interested, but active involvement – that's another story. People won't do what there isn't a time code for, and the bosses won't assign time codes for activities that are not directly involved in making money. If it isn't a part of the employee training plan, employees would have to work on it in the evenings. But why would they do that? There wouldn't be any pay-off for it in this company. Too bad, the employees say. They'd have really liked to participate.

And so John, Margaret and Berry continue on their own. Slowly, they begin to get a grasp on the notion of architecture and what its value could be for their company. Things continue like that for a while. John, Margaret and Berry have the feeling that they are making good progress. But they are concerned that the rest of the organization cannot be brought onside.

At the time of the annual performance appraisal interviews, John goes into the interview with his manager, Peter Miller, full of confidence. It is a great surprise to John that Peter is not at all satisfied. Wasn't John supposed to deliver an architecture? Where is it? John explains that delivering an architecture is not something that you can just do. It takes time! Many more people will have to become involved. To do it properly, the organization must collectively adopt a process of architectural thinking. You must not think of architecture as a product but as a continuous process.

Peter is not pleased with this answer. That wasn't the deal. Everything sounds so vague. Peter needs to see concrete goals and milestones. What else can he evaluate? As he sees it, things have not gone well. It won't count for this year's evaluation, but he wants to see John come up with some concrete milestones for the coming six months. Otherwise, John could better spend his time on other activities.

## White Architects in a Yellow Organization

Albert Johnson, senior information analyst in the retail division, has become enthusiastic about architecture. He went to a conference on architecture, heard about DYA and is convinced that his organization could find it extremely useful. As soon as he returns to work he talks animatedly about it with his colleagues, hoping to ignite their enthusiasm. There is certainly room for structural improvements in their work procedures; surely they want to work on that.

Enthusiastically, Albert assembles a group of fellow employees. Every Friday afternoon at four they meet to discuss architecture and to investigate what they can do about it themselves. There are many opportunities, so they get down to work. They begin small by streamlining their own activities using templates, structures and approaches that they collectively develop. Before long they are attracted to the notion of components, which they can see will make their information supply more flexible. They conceptualize distinct components and share their models with their immediate colleagues. Gradually they win an increasing number of supporters for their ideas.

Suddenly, the edict comes down from management: we are converting to an ERP package.

Why an ERP package? That doesn't fit with the notion of components. What do you mean by components? How are they involved? Everyone is switching to ERP. We cannot allow ourselves to fall behind.

This is certainly a jolt for Albert and his group. They had things well in hand, and then along comes management with such a worthless idea. But hey, things aren't that bad. We'll just keep on with what we're doing. An ERP package is not going to work here. While a grandiose program is set up in the organization to implement ERP, Albert and his cohorts happily continue along developing their component architecture.

Although things are never so black and white, situations like those described above will certainly be recognizable to many people. However, when you find yourself in such a situation, it is often difficult to determine exactly where things are going wrong. In these cases, the five-color model provides an excellent tool for gaining better insight into the underlying circumstances. This manner of thinking in color also helps to determine how improvements can be implemented to produce the right blend of colors.

For more information about the color model of thinking, we refer you to De Caluwé and Vermaak [5].

# REFERENCES

1. Berg, M. van den and M. van Steenbergen, "Niveaus in werken onder architectuur," *Informatie* (March 2003).
2. Bloem, J., M. van Doorn and P. Mittal, *Making IT Governance Work in a Sarbanes–Oxley World*, John Wiley & Sons, 2005.
3. Boeters, A. and B. Noorman, *Kwaliteit op maat, IT-projecten beheersen met de RADAR-methode*, Ten Hagen en Stam, 2003.
4. Butler Group, *Enterprise Architecture: An End-to-End Approach for Re-aligning IT with Business Aims*, 2004.
5. Caluwé, L. de and H. Vermaak, *Learning to Change: A Guide for Organization Change Agents*, Sage, 2003.
6. Delden, P. van, *Professionals, kwaliteit van het beroep*, Contact, 1995.
7. IEEE Std 1471-2000. *IEEE Recommended Practice for Architectural Description of Software-Intensive Systems*, 2000.
8. Goldratt, E.M. and J. Cox, *The Goal: A Process of Ongoing Improvement*, second edition, Gower, 1993.
9. Greefhorst, D., H. Koning and H. van Vliet, "De dimensies in architectuurbeschrijvingen", *Informatie* (November 2003).
10. Hofstede, G., *Allemaal andersdenkenden: Omgaan met cultuurverschillen*, Contact, 1995.
11. Hoogervorst, J.A.P., "*Enterprise Architecture: Enabling Integration, Agility and Change*," Paper LAC2003.
12. Koop, R., R. Rooijmans and M. de Theye, *Regatta®, ICT-implementaties als uitdaging voor een vier-met-stuurman*, Ten Hagen en Stam, 2003.
13. Kwakman, F. and A. Postema, *Het team als probleemoplosser, de moderatiemethode*, Kluwer, 1996.
14. Mastenbroek, W., *Verandermanagement*, Holland Business Publications, 1997.
15. METAgroup, *Diagnostic for Enterprise Architecture*, META Practice, October 2001.
16. METAgroup, *Enterprise Planning & Architecture Strategies Research Trends for 2003/2004*, 2004.
17. Paras, G., *Architecture Readiness Assessment*, METAgroup, 1999.
18. Paras, G., *Just Enough Architecture, Just in Time*, METAgroup Delta 2365, July 2003.
19. Raadt, B. van der, J. Soetendal, M. Perdeck and H. van Vliet, "*Architectuur is een tweestromenland*," Paper LAC2003.
20. Rijsenbrij, D., J. Schekkerman and H. Hendrickx, *Architectuur, besturingsinstrument voor adaptieve organisaties*, Lemna, 2002.

21. Schekkerman, J., *How to Survive in the Jungle of Enterprise Architecture Frameworks*, Trafford, 2003.
22. Truijens, J. and T. de Gouw, "Architectuur en alignment," *Informatie* (November 2002).
23. United States General Accounting Office, *Information Technology: A Framework for Assessing and Improving Enterprise Architecture Management*, Version 1.1, April 2003.
24. Veld, J. in 't, *Analyse van organisatieproblemen, Een toepassing van denken in systemen en processen*, Stenfert Kroese, 1990.
25. Wagter, R., M. van den Berg, J. Luijpers and M. van Steenbergen, *Dynamic Enterprise Architecture: How to Make IT Work*, John Wiley & Sons, 2005.
26. Westbrock, T., *Architecture Process Maturity Revisited and Revised*, METAgroup Delta 2902, May 2004.
27. Wierdsma and Swieringa, *Lerend organiseren, Als meer van hetzelfde niet helpt*, Stenfert Kroese, 2002.

# INDEX

# ABOUT THE AUTHORS

This book is written by two principal consultants enterprise architecture of Sogeti Nederland B.V. In this capacity they have advised and supported many organizations and companies in different countries all over the world. Among them the authors share many years of experience in the field of enterprise architecture. The book is based on these experiences as well as on the experiences of many other professionals in the field. The authors have brought together some twenty of these professionals in an architectural community that convenes three times a year to discuss actual themes in the field of enterprise architecture.

The authors also converted their knowledge into workshops and courses of various depths and breadths. In addition they frequently present the material contained in the book to companies as well as professional organizations.

They put their knowledge also to use by performing assessments of the state of the enterprise architectural processes within organizations.

### Martin van den Berg

Martin van den Berg is an architecture service line manager at Sogeti Nederland B.V. In this role he is responsible for the development of architecture services and expertise in Sogeti. Additionally he provides guidance to organizations in the professionalization of working with architecture. He is one of the founders of DYA and co-author of *Dynamic Enterprise Architecture, How to Make It Work*.

Martin van den Berg is also chairman of the architecture section of the Dutch Computer Society. Martin has published several articles and is a much sought after speaker at architecture seminars.

### Marlies van Steenbergen

Marlies van Steenbergen is principal consultant enterprise architecture at Sogeti Nederland B.V. As such, she has guided many organizations in the implementation of an effective enterprise architecture practice. She also transfers her experience and knowledge in the field of architecture by coaching architects and architecture teams. Marlies van Steenbergen is one of the founders of DYA and co-author of *Dynamic Enterprise Architecture, How to Make It Work*. She chairs Sogeti's Architectural Competence Network. Marlies has published several articles and is a frequent speaker at architecture seminars both at home and abroad.

# ABOUT THE SERIES

The new enterprise requires a new type of leadership based on the logical continuation of historical effort, while not doing what has been done just because it has been done that way in the past. Agility and leadership when combined is a cohesive presentation of common sense mined from the few truly successful projects as opposed to the aggregation of every (predominately failed) effort declared complete not only successful projects but projects that really add value to a business imperative. We are living in a new era where one seeks uncommon approaches while maintaining common virtues.

The art of leadership is about knowing and influencing people so that they can come to share common values resulting in more efficiency in achieving the strategic vision for the enterprise. Leadership must also embrace diversity which will lead to a much more lively dialectic.

The Enterprise Series has earned its place as a valuable resource to those who want to ramp up quickly and stay ahead of the curve. The authors of books within this series are not writers hired to cover the "hot" topic of the minute. Instead they are thought leaders and expert practitioners who bring insight to the community at large based on real-world experience. More importantly, they are not theorists but actually practice what they preach.

This series is founded on the conviction that enterprises should differentiate themselves, their architecture and their people based on the way they think as much as on the products or services they sell. Thought leadership is all about time-honored expertise and comprehensive capabilities. Its inflection point however is new thinking and original perspectives.

We hope you find this series and this book to be a practical guide and trusted advisor leading you successfully on your journey.

James McGovern
Rajanish Dass
Anthony Finkelstein
John Gøtze

# THE ENTERPRISE SERIES

J. McGovern, O. Sims, A. Jain and M. Little: *Enterprise Service Oriented Architectures.*
Concepts, Challenges, Recommendations. 2006        ISBN 1-4020-3704-X
M. van den Berg and M. van Steenbergen: *Building an Enterprise Architecture Practice.* Tools,
Tips, Best Practices, Ready-to-Use Insights. 2006       ISBN 1-4020-5605-5

springer.com